Awesome Ancient Ancestors

by Elizabeth Levy

Illustrated by Daniel McFeeley

with Additional Material by J. R. Havlan

SCHOLASTIC INC.

New York Toronto London Auckland Sydney
Mexico City New Delhi Hong Kong Buenos Aires

Scholastic gratefully acknowledges the original inspiration of
Terry Deary's *Horrible Histories* series, published by
Scholastic Publications Ltd., London, U.K.

Library of Congress Cataloging-in-Publication Data

Levy, Elizabeth
Awesome ancient ancestors / by Elizabeth Levy; illustrated by Daniel
McFeeley; with additional material by J.R. Havlan
p. cm. — (America's horrible histories)
Includes index.
ISBN 0-439-30349-4
1. Indians of North America — Antiquities — Juvenile literature. 2. Indians of
Mexico — Antiquities — Juvenile literature. 3. North America — Antiquities
— Juvenile literature
[1. Indians of North America — Antiquities. 2. Indians of Mexico —
Antiquities.] I. McFeeley, Dan, ill. Havlan, J.R. III. Title.

E77.92 .L48 2001
970.01 — dc21   2001020424

12 11 10 9 8 7 6 5 4 3 2 1   1 2 3 4 5 6/0

Printed in the U.S.A.   37

First Scholastic paper-over-board printing, September 2001

www.Elizabeth Levy.com

To Professor Forrest McDonald, Distinguished Professor of American History at the University of Alabama, who many, many years ago taught me that history was juicy, full of life, and certainly wacky. I learned more about good writing from his example and from his history class than I learned anywhere else. — E. L.

Acknowledgments

Thanks to Professor Terry Harrison from the New York University Department of Anthropology, who patiently read this manuscript and answered my questions as it kept changing and changing. To April Hamel, who read the manuscript and added a subtle humor to it. To David Shayne of *MAD* magazine for his quick wit and added jokes. Finally, heartfelt thanks again to Jean Feiwel and Sheila Keenan, who saw this book through its first growing pains, and who realized that sometimes hitting your funny bone can make you say "ouch."

Expert Readers: Terry Harrison, Professor of Anthropology, New York University; Shannon Rothenberger, Anishinaabe/Michif

What's So Funny?

History is usually a random, messy affair . . .
Mark Twain, *A Horse's Tail*

The one who tells the stories rules the world.
Hopi saying

Humor and history have a lot in common. They let everybody in on the joke about how funny, impossible, clever, misguided, smart, or silly humans can be and have always been. History and jokes can be horrible and wacky, often at the same time. Horrible comes from the Latin word *horree*, which means to bristle, to make your hairs stand on end. Wacky comes from the old English word *thwack*, from the sound a stick would make smacking something or someone. So, at the very least, the wacky and horrible parts of history will wake you up.

There's a saying that if you don't know your own history, you are condemned to repeat it. I say that if we can't laugh at ourselves, we're in even worse trouble. There are facts and jokes in this book that will make you laugh out loud, ones that will make you grin and groan, and ones that will make you squirm.

4

The joke below dates from the Maya era, which means it's so old it has mold on it — but real people told it, real people laughed at it. So while you're laughing at this and all the other jokes and cartoons in *Awesome Ancient Ancestors*, don't forget that the information here is real, at least as far as anybody knows. Just remember, historians keep learning, and ideas about what really happened in the past sometimes change as quickly as most people change their underwear.

What hums while it smacks you, but you can't see it?

The wind.

Search for History's Lost Jokes

TIME LINE

BCE stands for **B**efore the **C**ommon **E**ra, which is anytime before the year 1. CE stands for **C**ommon **E**ra, which is anytime from the year 1 forward.

100,000 years ago to 10,000 years ago — North America in ice age

??? to 10,500 BCE People arrive in the Americas; they hunt, fish, gather plants, build houses, and barbecue

9500 to 8500 BCE Clovis people hunt with great-looking spear points; people spread out

9000 to 8200 BCE Folsom people hunt with even greater-looking spear points

By 7000 BCE Ice age ends; big mammals disappear

By 5000 BCE Corn planted in Mexico, squash and pumpkins in the United States

1800 to 500 BCE Unknown people build huge earthworks in Louisiana

1200 BCE The Olmecs build cities in Mexico

700 to 100 BCE The Adena build mounds in Ohio

400 BCE Olmec Empire declines

Around 100 BCE to 500 CE Hopewell people build mounds in Ohio

0 to 750 CE Teotihuacán, one of the largest cities in the ancient world, rises in Mexico

Around 300 CE The Maya Empire in its "classic" period in Mexico

603 to 683 CE King Pakal the Great, Maya king, reigns

600 to 1300 CE The Effigy and Mississippi Mound cultures arise

700 to 1000 CE The Hohokam culture in Arizona at its height

750 to 900 CE The Maya Empire declines, so does the city of Teotihuacán

800 CE Corn planted east of Mississippi River; Mississippi Mound Builders at work

By 900 CE Cities and roads built in Chaco Canyon, New Mexico

1000 CE One of biggest pyramids in the world built in Cahokia, opposite St. Louis

Contents

Introduction

Ancient America wasn't a wilderness when the Europeans arrived. By the time Columbus got to what came to be called the "New World," North Americans already had a history that dated back more than 13,000 years. They had empires and great cities, and one of the largest pyramids in the world was smack-dab across the Mississippi River from present-day St. Louis.

My ancestors and I have been walking on that beach for about 13,000 years.
I wonder what he thinks is so new?

North America is huge. It's a nine-million-square-mile continent that includes Canada, the United States, and Mexico. It goes from the Arctic Circle down to Panama — and ancient Americans found ways to live in all of it. They developed thousands of cultures and left behind thousands of stories originally told in more than 1,000 languages. The ancient history of North America isn't as well known as the ancient history of Greece, Egypt, or Rome, but it is just as old and just as extraordinary.

It's hard to know what to call the people who made that history. The first North Americans probably had thousands of different names for themselves, but because there are so few written

We just wanted to welcome you to the neighborhood!

records, no one knows what these names were. Whoever they were and however they arrived during the ice age, they were newcomers compared to the cockroaches, mammoths, and dinosaurs that had been here long before them.

Let's just call them ancient Americans. Ancient means old. Very old. As in you're so old, a saber-toothed cat had you for breakfast. After all, saber-toothed cats were definitely here to greet and eat the first Americans.

Hard as it is to figure out what to call ancient Americans, it's even harder to tell the whole

story of ancient America. Like most periods in ancient history, this was a time when few people wrote anything down. There's lots of disagreement about what really happened in ancient North America, but one thing everyone agrees on — it all started a long, long, long, long time ago. . . .

Elizabeth Levy

Hello again, everybody

Mel Roach here. I'm back to guide you through another exciting time in history. No, it's not the time your first baby tooth fell out or the time you took the training wheels off your bike. I'm talking about the time period when humans decided to take matters into their own hands — or more specifically, into their own mouths.

You see, there came a time in very ancient history when people figured out that some food tastes better when it's cooked. You might be thinking, *"Well, duh!,"* but remember: People were hanging around this continent a long, long time ago, way before there were electric ovens, microwaves, toasters, or even a McDonalds! (Can you imagine?) Back then, cooking was news — especially to the prehistoric animals that got cooked!

But early humans didn't just have barbecues.

They also learned how to grow food and then whip up tasty dishes from what they had grown. Corn was their favorite. Can you believe that? A *vegetable* was among the ancient Americans' favorite food! People grew corn almost everywhere and ate it almost all the time. Luckily, some of these ancient ancestors also figured out how to make even tastier food, like chocolate and . . . more chocolate! Who needs anything else? Ancient people didn't just fill their bellies, though, they also filled their minds. They invented writing, created art, played sports, built cities, and threw feasts for their friends where everybody ate a lot! When I think of all those crumbs . . . yum!!!

So, find a comfortable seat and settle in. Maybe grab a snack; a nice bit of chocolate or an ear of corn goes well with this all-true, all-amazing story of ancient America.

Chapter 1
Hello, People! Good-bye, Mammoths

Picture yourself as one of the first kids ever to arrive in North America! It's toward the end of the ice age. It's chilly, but where the glaciers end, the place is teeming with animals. Mastodons use their trunks to gently nosh their way through the forests. Giant ground sloths are so huge, you would fit in one of their paws (not that you'd want to!). Rats are the size of baby cows. Woolly rhinoceroses and woolly mammoths lumber through the grasslands, with thick coats and

TIME LINE

100,000 to 9000 BCE Glaciers cover much of North America	**???** People arrive in what is now North America; nobody is sure exactly when	**10,500 BCE** Humans definitely in the Americas; they have settled in Monte Verde, Chile

14

thicker layers of fat to keep them warm. Camels and horses roam freely in the grasslands and American deserts. They share the grasslands with mammoths nearly the size of tractor trailers and bison that stand seven feet high at the hump and have horns that measure six feet from

The Dating Game

Prom dates, double dates, blind dates, dates in ancient history. They can all be horrible to figure out. People around the world keep track of time and dates in different ways. Scholars generally now write dates as BCE for Before the Common Era, which is anytime before the year 1; or CE for Common Era, which is anytime from the year 1 forward (we live in the Common Era). Think of a big number line where 1 is in the middle: everything to its left is BCE; 1 and everything to its right is CE. If all these dates give you a headache, you're not alone. The dating game isn't easy. Just ask anyone who's tried it.

Around 9000 BCE
Clovis people leave their spear points all over North America; they barbecue mammoths and also eat lots of other tasty food

8000 to 7000 BCE
North America gets warmer; the mammoths and other ice-age mammals disappear

2,000 CE
Scientists want to clone a mammoth, proving that everything old is new again

No, YOU can be the first kid in America.

No, I insist!

AMERICAS

No, no, no! You first!

tip to tip. Preying on all these animals are dire wolves and saber-toothed cats that slice open their prey's bellies with razor-sharp front teeth.

If you were that first American kid, looking out at what would eventually be called America, it would have looked like the African savanna when Africa was full of animals. The big mystery is where did *you* come from and when? And why, after you saw all those huge, dangerous animals, did you decide to stay?

Who Was the First American Settler?

The truth is that nobody really knows when or even how people first arrived on this continent. One thing scientists do know for sure is that people came a long time ago, and they didn't pull up in a minivan!

Most scientists believe that *Homo sapiens* came from Africa and spread out across the world around 100,000 to 50,000 years ago. At that time, the Earth was going through an ice age. Humans seem to have an innate curiosity to see what's around the next mountain or just beyond that next glacier. Scientists used to think that the Americas were the last stop on *Homo sapiens'* world tour.

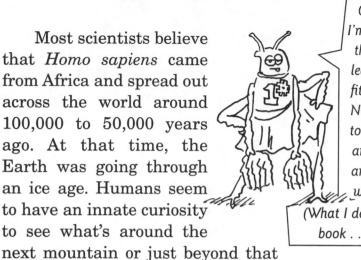

O.K. . . . I'm wearing the cheer-leader out-fit. But I'm NOT going to jump up and down and yell "I was #1!" (What I do for this book . . . oy.)

Theory 147: How People Got to America

Give us a call when you get there.

During the coldest periods of the ice age, so much ocean water was locked up in ice that there was a 1,000-mile-wide land strip between Asia and Alaska. (Many people call this the Beringia Bridge, even though it really wasn't a bridge but was actually the floor of what is today the Bering Sea.) For a long time, scholars thought that the first Americans crossed over Beringia on foot from Siberia to Alaska around 10,000 BCE, probably following and hunting the huge mammoths.

In the 1990s, scholars called archaeologists

Happy Birthday, Dear Mammoth. How Old Are You Now?

How do scientists know that mammoths and saber-toothed cats were in America at the same time as humans? One good clue is that they've found spear points made by humans in mammoth bones. Still, how do they know exactly when that mammoth was alive? In 1949, while studying the atom bomb, Dr. Willard Libby got the Nobel prize for discovering radiocarbon 14. All living things, you included (and, of course, that mammoth), have radiocarbon in them. When we die, this carbon starts decaying bit by bit. It's kind of like swallowing an hourglass. Because it decays at a steady rate, radiocarbon 14 can be used to accurately date bones and charcoal up to 100,000 years old.

Other tools and technology have helped researchers in the 50 years since Dr. Libby's discovery. Scientists found some of the earliest houses in either of the Americas at the very tip of South America. Archaeologists may sound like folks who spend a lot of time under McDonalds' golden arches munching hamburgers, but *archaeo* is Greek for ancient, and *logo* means to study. So archaeologists study ancient people. The shelters they found in Monte Verde, Chile, rocked the world of archaeology. Radiocarbon showed that these houses made of bones and covered with animal hides are definitely from at least 10,500 BCE.

can now extract chemicals from bones to find out what that mammoth ate. Some scientists are even hoping to clone a frozen mammoth from its DNA. Scientists also trade information on the Internet and at international conventions.

Some Other Uses for Radiocarbon Dating

Ma'am, I wouldn't buy that milk if I were you.

Some minute bits of carbon from a fire at the site might even be 30,000 years old. Archaeologists couldn't figure out how, if humans had just arrived in North America from Beringia, they got down south to Chile so fast. Keep in mind, they couldn't hop on a jet plane.

Alternate Routes: The Top Theories

The discoveries in Monte Verde and elsewhere opened up the debate on how and when humans arrived in the Americas. There are lots of theories. Scientists love Greek and Latin words; theory comes from the Greek word for spectator, or someone who views something and tries to make sense of what he or she is seeing. Watching dueling scientists argue about who was the first ancient American is a great spectator sport.

1. **People crossed the Pacific Ocean.** The ancient people who settled the Pacific Islands had long canoes. Perhaps they paddled to the Americas. They could have arrived anytime, not only during the era when Beringia was above water.

2. **They crossed the Atlantic Ocean.** In Virginia, South Carolina, and Pennsylvania, archaeologists have found stone tools that may be more than 20,000 years old. Both North America and Europe were still deep in the ice

age then. The Atlantic Ocean must have been full of huge floating icebergs. A few archaeologists think people in small boats may have come over from Europe or North Africa, hugging the coasts and hopping from iceberg to iceberg along the way.

3. **They crossed the Beringia Bridge early!**
Currently, many scientists believe that humans
did cross over the Beringia Bridge, but that they
arrived much earlier than previously thought.
The only time that the Beringia Bridge would
have been dry land solid enough for people to
walk on it was either 75,000 to 45,000 years ago
or 25,000 to 12,000 years ago; both periods are
clearly earlier than 10,000 BCE.

4. **People have been here since the beginning.** Some of the oldest creation stories
passed down from the first peoples in the
Americas say that humans have been here
since the beginning of time. Many myths tell of
the first humans' difficult climb up to Earth.
Others tell of Sky Woman, mother of the first

people. She plunged to Earth but was saved through the efforts of an Earth Diver. An Earth Diver is an animal that went down under the primeval water to fetch mud and form land to break Sky Woman's fall. In many myths, this animal is a turtle (the Lenape and the Iroquois call North America "Turtle Island").

Bears? Turtles? Come on, get real, guys. If anybody was here at the beginning, you know it was a cockroach!

Sometimes the Earth Diver is a bear with mud in its paw. In these ancient accounts, the mud grows and grows into the hills, valleys, mountains of the Earth, and eventually life on Earth begins.

There is really only one thing archaeologists know for sure about the first humans in the Americas: They spread out. Spear points and remains of ancient Americans have been found everywhere from New Mexico to South Carolina, from Idaho to Pennsylvania. For people who had to walk everywhere, they sure got around.

Clovis Hunters

In 1932, in a place called Blackwater Draw, near Clovis, New Mexico, a road construction crew dug up a gravel pit along the shores of a lake that had dried up long ago. They found a spear point, and next to it a really big animal tooth. Luckily, they called in experts to look at their finds. The experts dug even deeper and found the fossil bones of a mammoth with a spear point actually stuck in it.

Great! I'm glad you guys find this sooooo interesting!

This was the first time that scientists could prove that humans had actually been in North America at the same time as the mammoths. It was also proof that humans and mammoths weren't exactly the best of friends. Archaeologists came to call these particular ancient Americans the Clovis people, for the town in New Mexico where the road crew had found the first spear point. The odds are about a trillion to one that the ancient Americans of New Mexico called themselves "Clovis people." Nonetheless, Clovis is the name given to the bands of people who spread out over North

America at the end of the ice age.

Thousands of Clovis spear points have been found in Kentucky, Tennessee, and Alabama. In fact, Clovis spear points have been found in every one of the 48 states of the lower United States, as well as in Canada and Mexico. No one knows exactly how many Clovis people there were, but archaeologists estimate that there were probably fewer than a million people in both North and South America around 8000 BCE.

Sharp and to the Point

Most Clovis spear points were incredibly sharp killing tools. These two- to six-inch-long spear points were beautifully made, with carefully chipped edges. When modern scientists tried to replicate a Clovis point, it took them years to figure out how to do it.

The Clovis people chose incredibly hard, glassy stones, like flint, jasper, or quartz, for their spear points. A few spear points discovered were made out of obsidian. Obsidian is a shiny black volcanic glass that is almost as strong and sharp as a diamond. Clovis people probably traded with one another for these different stones and spear points. Spear points found in northeastern Colorado and in Washington State were made of stones that came from as far away as Texas. Because the Clovis didn't have mail service or overnight express, that means somebody had to bring those stones around.

The Clovis people also invented a spear thrower now called an "atlatl" after a weapon the

Aztecs used many thousands of years later. The atlatl had a hook on the end, kind of like a dart thrower or a missile launcher. The atlatl was hollow, so the shaft of the spear fit into it. The hunter launched the spear with the atlatl.

Other tools have also been found along with the Clovis spear points — tools for cutting and slicing meat and for mashing up food. Of course, nobody knows exactly everything the Clovis people ate. Several spear points have been found near mammoth bones, but Clovis people also hunted bison, caribou, deer, bears, horses, camels, and even rabbits.

Because so many spear points have been found, for a long time many history books portrayed ice-age Americans as people who did almost nothing but hunt. That wasn't the whole picture, not by a long shot (or a long spear throw). The Clovis people also had wooden sticks for digging out roots. They discovered those plants and berries that were good to eat. They found out which plants made you sick or even killed you. Of course, they had to get sick and maybe die to find out, but that's life . . . or death!

Eventually, the Clovis people braided grass and reeds and developed baskets and bark containers to carry the plants that they picked. These were like the first shopping bags, only they didn't have supermarket names printed on them. People also used other plants to weave clothing.

Weird Diets Not to Try at Home

The earliest humans did not have an easy time figuring out what to eat. Most wild plants and wild animals are either not safe to eat or don't taste good to humans. Scientists believe that most humans want to eat only about one percent of all animals and plants. Scientists under 12 years of age believe that most humans want to eat only .009 percent of cafeteria food.

Top Six Reasons Not to Eat Something:

1. It's too hard on the stomach. Don't try eating tree bark.
2. It's poisonous. Don't try eating a monarch butterfly or a death-cap mushroom.
3. It's yucky. Lots of people would put jellyfish in this category.
4. A lot of wild foods take too much time and work, such as very small nuts. (This does not include your little brother.)
5. It's hard to catch enough of them to make a meal — take bugs, for example.
6. The food is very dangerous to hunt. Think rhinoceros.

Inventions like baskets and pottery helped people gather even more plants. Thousands of years later, plant knowledge would lead to farming, and farming changed the Earth much more than hunting did. Still, baskets and wooden planting sticks don't last as long as stone spears. They're not lying around for road crews to find. So for a long time, history books and museums didn't show much about the gathering side of what archaeologists call "gathering and hunting."

Uh-oh, Major Extinction Ahead!

Something very strange happened at the end of the last ice age, just as the Clovis people were spreading out. All the many different kinds of mammoths — not just the woolly mammoths — disappeared. This was an extinction as dramatic as the great dinosaur wipeout 65 million years ago — but no comet hit Earth. This last extinction drives scientists crazy because it happened only 10,000 years ago. They can't figure it out.

It wasn't just the mammoths that died out. Many, many large animals became extinct. Lucky for humans, we weren't one of them. The mastodons that lived in the forests became extinct. The saber-toothed cats that dined on the big beasts (and probably plenty of humans) also died out. The giant sloths disappeared. Horses

You can sometimes see archaeologists in action at the **Blackwater Draw Museum** in Clovis, New Mexico. Museum exhibits show how the Clovis people might have hunted. The **Montana Historical Society Museum** in Helena, Montana, has many Clovis spear points and atlatls as part of its "First People" exhibit. The **Burke Museum of Natural History and Culture,** in Seattle, Washington, has some of the largest Clovis spear points ever found. Children can try to attach replica Clovis spear points to spear shafts. The **Cahokia Mounds Spear-Throwing Contest** in Cahokia, Illinois: As part of an ancient American festival, there is often a spear-throwing demonstration open to both children and adults. In fact, there are many atlatl-throwing contests throughout the United States and Canada.

disappeared from North America until the Spaniards brought them back 10,000 years later.

For two million years in North America, the glaciers had come and gone, and each time all these animals survived. This time they didn't. Although this mass extinction happened all over the world, in North America it seems more animals died out than anywhere

else. It's one of the greatest mysteries of pre-history and it *still* isn't solved. Naturally, there are a lot of theories.

Many scientists believe the warmer weather caused the extinction, but the giant mammals had already survived many changes of weather and climate. Other scientists point out that the only apparent difference this time was that there were people like the Clovis in America. Some scientists believe that the humans hunted so many animals that eventually many species became extinct. Other scholars think this was physically impossible. Still another extinction theory says that giant animals in the Americas might have died because they couldn't fight off the germs carried by humans.

However the extinction happened, life in the Americas was never the same. The earliest Americans must have liked some of the changes. They were in less danger of being eaten. More important, they were in less danger of freezing to death. Warm weather, spears, or germs, whichever theory is correct, there is no doubt about one thing: By around 7000 BCE, horses and camels were gone and the great mammoth feast was over. If people were going to survive in the Americas, they were going to have to figure out how to get along without mammoth meat for barbecues, mammoth bones for houses, and mammoth skins for clothing. Without horses, life in North America was going to be very different from the way people in the rest of the world lived. North Americans were on their own.

Now they've

gone and done it. Can you imagine life without mammoth barbecues? I sure can't. Not to mention the fact that now people won't have a thing to wear.

Personally, I'm still wondering how humans got here in the first place. Did they walk over a frozen land bridge? Paddle across the Pacific? Hop across the Atlantic? Or fly first-class? Your guess is as good as mine. (But just between you and me, I bet flying first-class isn't the answer.)

One thing seems pretty clear, though: People killed off a lot of ice-age mammals using those nasty weapons they invented. A spear? Yikes! An atlatl? I don't know what kind of name-name that is-is, but it sure sounds funny-funny.

But, you know, pretty soon people found out that mammoths and mastodons weren't the only tasty, furry animals on Earth. Humans got lucky!

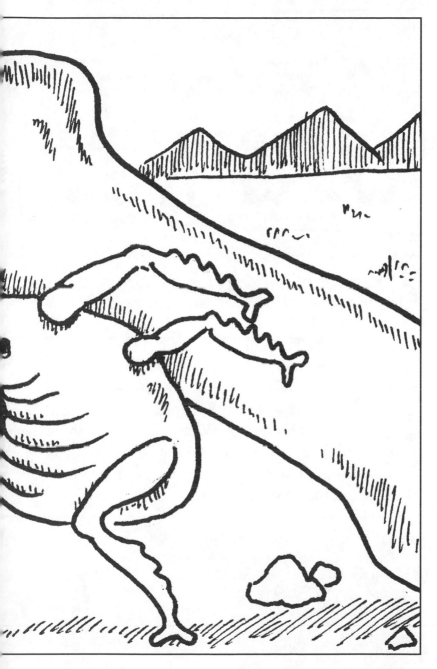

Chapter 2

A Huntin' and Gatherin' We Will Go

Around 10,000 years ago, the glaciers slowly began to melt. It turned warm again in North America, just as it had several times before, during the ice age. The glaciers that covered most of North America thawed. All that water locked up in ice began to melt. Water flowed back into the sea. Beringia, the land between Siberia and Alaska, was underwater. Whatever way people got here, they were now blocked off from walking back to Asia. Humans and ice-age mammals were locked together in a new, warmer land. Talk

TIME LINE

10,000 to 7000 BCE
The end of the last ice age; Beringia disappears under rising oceans

9000 to 8200 BCE
Folsom people hunt bison from Canada to Texas

Around 7400 BCE
The Kennewick man and the Spirit Cave man of Nevada are both alive

36

Glub, Glub, Glub: Myths About Floods

People from all around the world have ancient stories that tell of Earth being flooded. Many ancient American creation myths say that in the beginning, there was no earth, only water. In one account, Coyote is floating on a small raft and gets lonely and asks the ducks to go under the water and bring up some mud with their webbed feet. Coyote then takes the mud and creates the world. *(Coyote is sometimes called the "Trickster." In modern legends, he even tricks archaeologists who try to make sense out of legends about him.)*

Among the ancient stories from other places in the world, there is the biblical flood story of Noah and his ark and an even older but similar Mesopotamian myth. The *Popul Vuh,* the sacred text of the Maya, also says, "Flood came from the sky, a great flood that fell." There are similar South Pacific, Chinese, and Greek flood myths. Archaeologists wonder if some of these myths may have been passed down by humans who were alive when the glaciers melted and much of the land was flooded. Humans had to sink or swim!

By 7000 BCE
Ancient Americans spread out all over North America; they survive by fishing, hunting, and gathering plants

5500 BCE
Some ancient Americans bury their dogs; archaeologists believe it shows the great respect they must have had for their pets

2000 CE
Modern Americans float giant balloons of dogs on their feast day, Thanksgiving; future archaeologists believe it shows great respect for their dogs

Thawing, freezing, thawing, freezing. Parka, swimsuit, parka, swimsuit. I wish somebody would make up his mind!

about being stranded! That's worse than being stuck in the principal's office all weekend.

Birds Got to Fly, Fish Got to Swim, People Got to Eat

When the mammoths and mastodons died out and other ice-age animals moved north, lots of animals rushed in to take advantage of all the good plants left to eat and the warmer weather. Deer spread out across North America. Elk and moose shared the woodlands with the deer. There were beavers, foxes, squirrels, rabbits, and lots of other small animals, too. Meanwhile, huge flocks of ducks and geese flew along the rivers and lakes. The rivers and oceans were full of fish.

After the glaciers melted, the ancient Americans continued to pick the tasty plants and to hunt and fish the tasty animals that thrived in the warmer environment. There was so much good food that for the most part they lived very well. They also got around!

By 9000 BCE, humans in North America were walking all over the same land where ice-age mammals had once roamed. The vast Pacific and Atlantic Oceans separated American humans from others of their kind. For thou-

sands of years, it appears that Americans had no contact with their cousins in other places on the globe. Not even so much as a card on their birthdays.

What was life really like for these ancient Americans who lived just after the ice age? People hunted caribou, deer, and small game that lived in the thick forests. On the Great Plains, they hunted the long-horned bison. Heavy rains from the melting snow flowed into streams and rivers that were filled with fish, so naturally people fished. In Boston, archaeologists have

found very intricate prehistoric fish traps that are at least 5,000 years old. Fish could swim into the traps, but they couldn't swim out.

Nothing Like a Nice Warm Cave

When the earliest Americans found a good place to live, like a warm cave, they tended to go back there again and again. Near Pittsburgh, Pennsylvania, there is a rock cave known as Meadowcroft. This cave is famous because people continued to picnic in it and seek protection in it until well into the 19th century. Radiocarbon dates show that people were living in that cave from at least 12,000 BCE — maybe as far back as 17,000 BCE or even earlier! Archaeologists think

Sorry, guys. We were here first.

Meadowcroft Rockshelter is less than an hour from downtown Pittsburgh. The Meadowcroft Museum tells the story of the site and its excavation. The cave itself is currently closed to visitors, but there are exhibits about the cave and life in prehistoric America. There are also amateur spear-throwing contests using an atlatl. **Russell Cave National Monument** is in Bridgeport, Alabama, near the border of Tennessee. Visitors can see the exposed cave wall rock layers, although much of the cave is still being excavated and is off-limits.

that after the ice age the woods around the cave would have been full of deer, rabbits, and other animals. The cave dwellers of Meadowcroft hunted, picked berries and nuts, and probably tried to avoid the poison ivy.

The cave-carving glaciers never reached the Southeast, but heavy rainfall sculpted huge caves in the area's limestone hills. At least 9,000 years ago, people were living in a place called Russell Cave near Bridgeport, Alabama. Russell Cave is huge. It goes back seven miles into the limestone. You could park a tractor trailer in its mouth. Men, women, and children camped on the rocky floor of this cave. Life there was a little nutty. People in Russell Cave ate so many nuts for so many thousands of years that there are deposits of nutshells that are 43 feet deep. Scientists have also found tools that must have been used to grind nuts. They found knife handles made out of bear teeth and a torch made from the hollowed leg bone of a bear.

Oh, Give Me a Home, Where the Buffalo Bison Roam

The biggest animal to survive the ice age was the bison. Bison weigh over 2,000 pounds. (If you ever see one, tell him he doesn't look a pound over 1,900; even bison enjoy being flattered.) With their big, beefy, hairy bodies and tough hides, bison have a remarkable resemblance to professional wrestlers.

Buffalo is just another word for bison. . . . then there's Buffalo, New York, the author Liz's hometown . . . and Liz's favorite baseball team, the minor league Buffalo Bisons.

Why did bison survive when so many other big ice-age mammals died off? Bison may not be the smartest animals on Earth, but they travel in herds and are among the best grass eaters. They can break down fiber that would make other animals burp themselves to death. Bison also had a longer mating season than most other ice-age mammals. This meant more bison babies were born.

42

How to Tell a Bison from a Professional Wrestler

Bison	Wrestler
Huge	Huge
Beefy	Beefy
Hard to bring down	Hard to bring down
Hairy Horns	Hairy underarms
	Only wears horns for big matches

Folsom Hunters

As the weather got warmer and the last of the glaciers melted, the Great Plains became green and grassy. All that yummy grass and no mammoths hogging it! The bison multiplied and multiplied until perhaps as many as 100 million of them grazed on the plains. With so many bison wandering around the Great Plains, it's no wonder

Honey, we're going to have another kid.

No problem. We eat grass.

Great! Another mouth to feed!

Oh, yeah.

that hunting bison became an ancient American way of life — one that lasted for thousands of years. Not an easy way of life, either. Even with a good spear, it was hard to bring down a bison. Ancient Americans had no horses to help them. They had to do it all on foot, although they did use dogs to help sniff out the herds and to pull sledges. The ancient bison hunters used a spear point that archaeologists call a Folsom point, and these people are called the Folsom people.

Oh, give me a home, where the giant bison roam and the . . . uh-oh!

How the Folsom Bison Hunters Got Their Name

In 1908, an African-American cowboy named George McJunkin found an ancient spear point when he was riding the range near the little town of Folsom, New Mexico. McJunkin saw that the spear point was still embedded in a giant bison bone. Because McJunkin found the spear point in Folsom, New Mexico, archaeologists call the first bison hunters — you guessed it, the Folsom people.

The Folsom spear points were smaller but just as well made as the Clovis spear points. (Like the Clovis spear points, Folsom spear points have been found all over North America: as far north as Montana, as far south as Mexico, and as far east as Alabama.) The Folsom used their spear points to hunt other game besides bison, such as deer or elk. Like the Clovis spear point, the Folsom spear point is considered a very fine killing tool. It was sharp enough to pierce an animal's thick hide, but its fluted sides didn't break when it hit bone. Folsom hunters also used the atlatl to help them throw their spears.

Folsom spear points were and are extremely difficult to make. Modern scholars and flint makers have gotten many bloody fingers trying to reproduce a Folsom point — and that's just from the paper cuts they got while drawing up the plans!

Our spear points take down the big guys so fast, sometimes you can't even get out of the way!

Folsom Museum in New Mexico has exhibits about George McJunkin and examples of Folsom spear points. The Folsom site itself is not open to the public.

How to Kill a Bison on Foot

Archaeologists wish they could go back and sit around a campfire with the Folsom hunters, but they can't. However, they are able to study the way that bison hunters in the 1800s hunted bison. Some of those hunters said that their hunting traditions and stories went all the way back to their oldest ancestors. These stories help archaeologists put together a picture of what Folsom hunters might have been like.

Before bison cliff drives, there were a few earlier hunting attempts—squirrel herding probably being the worst of them.

By 7000 BCE, ancient Americans had figured out ways to trap bison and drive whole herds over cliffs or into ravines. In both the United States and Canada, archaeologists have found ancient piles of boulders that lead to an edge of a cliff. The boulders were put there to guide the bison over the cliff. This technique of driving bison off cliffs was so successful that it would continue for nearly 10,000 years, until the 1800s.

What do you call a herd of bison going over a cliff? Bison droppings.

It sounds easy to kill bison by getting them to jump off a cliff, but it isn't. Bison can run at speeds of up to 35 miles per hour. Humans, even Olympic champs, can run only about 13 miles per hour. Although bison may not be the Albert Einsteins of the animal world, they are smart enough not to go off cliffs. They could easily have stepped around the boulders. So some hunters would try to guide the bison to the cliffs by dressing in buffalo skins. Others would stand alongside the boulders waving their hands to scare the bison and keep them moving toward the cliff. Still others were waiting at the bottom of the cliff with spears tied to Folsom points. If everything went all right (for the hunters, that is), up to 200 bison, each weighing more than 2,000 pounds, would stampede off the cliff, resulting in 400,000 pounds of bison stew.

After the Folsom hunters had killed the bison, they used almost every part of the animal. From bison skins, they made blankets, clothing, and roofs for their lodges. They made spoons and dishes out of bison horns. They stuffed cushions with the bison's shaggy hair. Even so, a lot of bison meat got wasted and rotted. Eventually,

Head-Smashed-In Buffalo Jump, in Fort Macleod, Alberta, Canada, is one of the best-preserved ancient American hunting sites. It's named for one of the dumbest ideas of all time. No, not karaoke. According to legend, Head-Smashed-In Buffalo Jump got its name because a young hunter wanted to see for himself what all those two-ton legs and horns looked like crashing down. This was a very dumb idea. The buffalo fell on the hunter's head, killing him. His smashed-in skull was found among all the buffalo bones, and that's how Head-Smashed-In got its name.

the descendants of the Folsom hunters figured out a recipe called pemmican. This dried bison meat lasted for a long time — a *very* long time. It was sort of like today's beef jerky, only it was made from real meat.

Dogs helped haul away the bison meat. The Folsom people most likely had dogs to help them when they stampeded the bison over the cliff. Even back then, a dog was a human's best friend.

Ancient Americans and Their Dogs

Dogs probably traveled with the first humans to America, perhaps sitting in their canoes, perhaps walking over the Beringia Bridge. With the horse and camel extinct, the dog was almost the only tame animal in ancient North America. Many early American legends tell of women and children being the first to tame dogs. There are even traditional jokes about dogs.

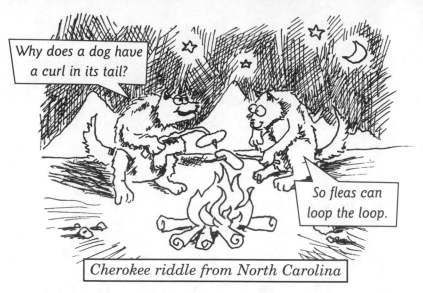

Cherokee riddle from North Carolina

Ancient dog burials have been found in New York, Florida, and Texas. Burial is almost always a sign of love and respect. Someone, nobody knows who, buried a little dog about the size of a fox terrier in a cave in Benton County, Missouri, about 5500 BCE. Archaeologists believe that these canine bones are among the earliest signs that prehistoric Americans honored their dogs. However, dogs were not only working pets, they were occasionally the source of meat and a course at a feast.

Ancient America's Food Court: Life Along the Pacific

The people of the Pacific Northwest are one of the greatest examples of successful gatherers and hunters. The Pacific Northwest was like the food court at the mall: plenty of food to choose from, all in one convenient location. The rivers in the

Northwest were full of salmon and other fish. The ocean was full of seals, whales, fish, and shellfish. The woods were full of berries and other plants as well as elks, bears, and deer. Archaeologists believe that the people of the Northwest led healthy lives for thousands of years by gathering and hunting. Gradually, they also developed important rituals and feasts. Some of these traditions have continued to this day.

Gee, honey, I don't know. It all looks so good.

In California, then as now, people had to adapt to a lot of different environments. (Just ask any actor who tries to make it in Hollywood.) In the foothills of the Sierra Nevada Mountains, people collected acorns and hunted deer, bears, and elks. On the islands off what is now San Diego, nearly 7,000 years ago, a new fishhook was invented. Using silvery abalone shells, the islands' ancient people created a hook shaped like a crescent moon. These glittery hooks turned out to be irresistible to fish. When archaeologists

studied the fish bones left on San Clemente Island, they were shocked by the number of fish that were caught. Literally thousands upon thousands of fish were snagged in a short period of time. Huge sheepshead fish, some weighing 37 pounds, were drawn in using those hooks. The islanders must have had amazing fish fries!

Diet Hints from the Earliest Americans

Most of what scientists know about the diet of the earliest Americans comes from very little evidence. Human bones are actually quite fragile, and ancient human skeletons often turn into dust. Only a few skeletons from just after the ice age have been found. The number of dinosaur fossils discovered far outnumber the remains of the earliest Americans. So far, the evidence seems to show that some of the earliest Americans were quite healthy and they had very few cavities (which made it very hard for prehistoric dentists to earn a living).

For example, the Spirit Cave man in Nevada is the oldest mummy ever found in North America; in fact, it's one of the oldest mummies in the world. New methods of radiocarbon dating prove that the Spirit Cave man was actually alive in 7515 BCE, making him much older than Egyptian mummies! The Spirit Cave man's bones are in good shape, showing that he had a healthy diet. However, he died because of an infected tooth, so maybe he *could* have used a prehistoric dentist.

The Spirit Cave man's mummified body was wearing moccasins and was wrapped in a grass shroud, showing that he had been specially prepared for burial and obviously well cared for when he died.

The remains of another ancient American were found recently in the 1990s by college students near Kennewick in Washington State. Archaeologists and newspaper articles have called him the Kennewick man. Preliminary radiocarbon dating shows that he was alive at around the same time as the Spirit Cave man, about 7000 BCE. The Kennewick man was not mummified and only his skeleton was found, none of his clothes. The Kennewick man has a

two-inch spear point in his pelvis. There's no way of knowing if he got it in a hunting accident, a fight, or a battle. Whatever way it happened, it's safe to assume he didn't want it there, though the Kennewick man survived with that spear in him for many years. He lived in good health until he was about 50, a sign that he most likely would have had help recovering from his injury.

Gathering and Hunting: Nice Work If You Can Get It

Scientists used to think that early gatherers and hunters led kind of sad lives, in which they were starving a lot of the time, except when they could catch big game. Although almost all ancient Americans hunted, outside of the Great Plains, where the huge bison herds roamed, ancient Americans probably gathered as much as they hunted. Until archaeologists took a close look at the bones and teeth of many of the earliest ancient Americans, they didn't realize just how many plants they ate. For example, potatoes, tomatoes, squash, and pumpkins grew in the Americas; they were unknown in the rest of the world until after Columbus.

So, ancient Americans hunted, fished, and ate their veggies. Archaeologists believe that these ancient Americans often needed only a few days a week to gather enough food. So what did they do with the rest of their time? Some of their ancient artworks give us mysterious clues.

One Possible Way Ancient Americans May Have Spent All That Free Time

C'mon, Dad. Swim faster!

Well, I don't

know about you guys, but I'm feeling pretty good about the way things are going for the humans. Something tells me that humans are going to survive just fine, and if there's anybody that knows about surviving, it's me. We cockroaches always know what's up. Now, if you'll excuse me, I've got to go. I have this weird feeling something bad is going down. Let's go see what those humans are doing with all that spare time on their hands. . . .

Chapter 3
Arty Ancient Americans

As the ancient Americans spread out, many of them lived together in groups, creating great monuments and colossal artworks that they would never have been able to do alone. Experts used to believe that people didn't start doing these activities, or living in towns, until they started farming. However, the more archaeologists study ancient American gatherers and hunters, the more they realize that prehistoric people lived very complicated lives — lives full of art, ritual, and feasting.

TIME LINE

Around 2500 BCE
Ancient Americans create elaborate rock art on canyon walls along the Pecos River in Texas and on rock outcroppings all over North America

1800 to 500 BCE
People along the Mississippi River create huge earthworks at Poverty Point, Louisiana

499 BCE
Price of earthworks skyrockets after people who built them pass away

58

It's bold, dynamic, and brimming with pathos. It evokes passion, yet it's strangely calm.

I call it "Hunting Guy."

You're self-taught, huh?

The Great Outdoor Art Gallery

Basically, the artistry of the Clovis people and the Folsom people can be seen only in their beautifully crafted tools. However, 4,000 years ago, ancient Americans in the Southwest began a tradition of using the canyon walls for painting dramatic visions that most likely had spiritual meanings.

Among the most sensational of these artworks are the huge figures painted above the Pecos River in Texas around 2500 BCE. These are some of the oldest paintings by North American artists that have yet been discovered. Very little is known about the people who created these paintings. Archaeologists have found no houses or bones that are as old as the paintings. Whoever these people were, among them were powerful artists. The most famous Pecos River painting is a bloodred, nine-foot cat, a cougar or panther that looks ready to pounce. Along with the panther, there are also other awesome drawings of humans, birds, and snakes.

The human figures are almost life-size. These pictures show them flinging their arms out wide. They are waving spears and clubs. Strange prickly ornaments are dangling from their arms and wrists. The ornaments probably represent cactuses. Some archaeologists think the human figures represent ancient spiritual leaders, responsible for communicating with the spirit world and guiding people from one world to the next. (If you go look at the paintings or any rock art, be careful. Falling off a canyon wall is a good way to go from one world to the next yourself.)

They paint cougars, mammoths, bison—never a cockroach. I tell ya, I just don't get no respect.

Rockin' Good Rock Art

So far at least 25,000 rock art sites have been found in the west and southwest United States. Almost all people who study prehistoric rock art admit that they do not know exactly what the drawings mean. Dating rock art is very difficult.

TRAVEL

The Pecos canyon drawings are located in **Seminole Canyon State Historical Park,** three and a half hours west of San Antonio, Texas. The panther painting and others can be viewed by tour only. Ancient drawings can be found all over the Southwest. **Petroglyph National Monument** in Albuquerque, New Mexico, is the only national monument created for the protection of rock art. **Signal Hill, Saguaro National Park West,** near Tucson, Arizona, has excellent examples of Hohokam rock art. (For more on these ancient Americans, see Chapter Seven.) Other great places to see rock art include **Valley of Fire State Park,** about an hour east of Las Vegas, Nevada; **Anasazi Coso Range,** about three hours north of Los Angeles, California; and **Canyonlands National Park,** about three hours south of Salt Lake City, Utah.

Glak! Hey, Glak! Hmmm . . . Wonder where he went?

Looks like Glak did a self-portrait here on the ground.

He is one lucky guy to have that kind of talent.

Now, just sign it and date it and you're finished.

What's today's date?

Who knows? Forget it, you're finished.

(Dating rock artists is notoriously difficult, too — just ask anyone who ever met one of the Rolling Stones.) Unless an ancient artist drew in charcoal, there is no radiocarbon dating for rock art. It's very hard for scientists to know exactly when the artist did the drawing.

What's Huge, Nearly 4,000 Years Old, and Shaped Like a Flying Bird?

Ancient Americans didn't just create art on canyon walls, they also created art out of the earth. One of the oldest of these earth sculptures at Poverty Point, Louisiana, is so huge that its size can really be appreciated only from the air. Weird, eh? It's not as if ancient art lovers had airplanes.

Poverty Point, just north of Vicksburg, Mississippi, is the oldest monumental earthwork and ceremonial gathering center in what is now the United States. Its six huge, moundlike ridges are built in a semicircle, as if they were an amphitheater. The 4,000-year-old mounds stretch for seven miles; one of them is spread out like the wings of a huge hawk. The wingspan is three-quarters of a mile long and 70 feet high.

Looking at Rock Art

There are two kinds of rock art. Pictographs are paintings on rock, and petroglyphs are cut right into the stone. Most rock art that has survived are petroglyphs, which are etched into canyon walls. If you ever find one of these cliff drawings or etchings, don't write or draw on top of it and don't try to chip it away and bring it home. You may be thinking, "*Duh,* who would do something stupid like that?" Lots of people have. Correction: lots of *stupid* people. A tremendous number of ancient drawings have been destroyed or stolen by looters. Sometimes even breathing on or touching an ancient rock painting can destroy it. Some of the cliff drawings are considered sacred, and these especially should be left alone. If you find some undiscovered rock art, tell someone who is in charge of the land you are visiting, a tribal elder, or someone at a museum or national park.

No, man, that's the Egyptians who put curses on the old art. There's none of that stuff here in North America.

Hey, people! You've got the beak waaaay too big!

Archaeologists believe Poverty Point might have been a place of religious worship. Clearly something major must have gone on there because many people worked very hard to create it. All the soil had to be moved by hand and carried in baskets. Archaeologists believe the Poverty Point ridges took five million work-hours to build! Nobody knows how many people worked on it.

Thousands of clay balls have been found in Poverty Point. Some of the balls are shaped like human figures; others are shaped like shells. Archaeologists believe that villagers used these balls to cook food in watertight baskets. First, the

Poverty Point State Commemorative Area in Epps, Louisiana, is located practically on the border between Mississippi and Louisiana, just north of Vicksburg, Mississippi. You can walk on trails around the mounds and visit a museum showing how the Poverty Point people might have lived.

clay balls were heated in a fire. Then, the hot balls were dropped into watertight baskets filled with water and food. The water heated up and the food cooked.

Until fairly recently, archaeologists thought that Poverty Point was a unique place. However, clay balls made and decorated in the "Poverty Point style" have been found as far away as Arkansas, Mississippi, Florida, Tennessee, and Missouri.

By about 1500 BCE, there might have been several thousand people living in Poverty Point. They were definitely traders. They got copper from the Great Lakes and stones from Alabama and Georgia. These ancient Americans probably knew where the best wild plants grew and may have gathered squash or pumpkins, but they didn't plow fields or plant crops. Around 700 BCE, however, people stopped living in Poverty Point. Nobody is exactly sure why. Meanwhile, huge cities were rising in Mexico and people there were farming. One of their crops changed life in the Americas for-ever — and caused a lot of corny jokes.

You think we've been at this for about 10 hours?

Yeah, I think so.

Cool! Only 4,499,990 more hours to go.

65

This story is really starting to get good, isn't it? Painting on walls, playing in the dirt, I told you these humans would be all right. In fact, I'd say they're better than just all right. People are fantastic! I've got to say, I really dig your art. That's right. Art. You see, art isn't just paintings or music or those weird statues on your neighbor's lawn. Art is anything someone creates to make you get all emotional when you look at it, or listen

to it, or touch it. Even that silly drawing your little brother made that your mom and dad taped to the refrigerator is art! Lots of ancient Americans hunted and gathered, fished, threw great feasts, and seem to have dug art. Some people really dug fields. Isn't that corny? Oops! Sorry. I gave it away. The crop that's coming that changed almost everybody's life was corn. . . . But you probably already figured that out, right?

Chapter 4
Swell Corn, Swelled Heads

Corn: the main source of food for many North Americans. Where did this essential crop come from? Sometime, probably around 5,000 years ago (some scholars think it was more like 9,000 years ago), people in Peru and Mexico began to plant corn. The first corncobs were just a couple of inches long, like the tiny ones you see at salad bars. The first corn growers learned to save and plant the seeds from the biggest cobs. Corncobs got bigger and bigger.

The Olmec people of what is now Mexico

TIME LINE

Anywhere from 7000 to 3000 BCE
Farmers plant corn, a plant that can't thrive without human help

Around 2500 BCE
The Olmecs farm and build villages along rivers of Mexico

1200 BCE
The Olmecs build great cities and create great art-work

68

were the first known great empire builders of North America. The Olmecs continued to fish, hunt, and gather wild plants, but they began planting corn as early as 2500 BCE along the Coatxalcoalcus River in Mexico. They also grew squash and beans, but corn became more and more important to them. Soon, they began to worship gods who would help them grow corn.

The new, bigger corn-cobs only grew if the Olmecs or other people planted them. Corn seeds stay in the husk unless picked out and saved by human hands. Scientists call a plant like this "domesticated," which comes from a Latin word, *domus*, meaning home. Domesticated means that a plant or animal lives with

Giant corn is great fun at picnics, but just try popping it for a movie!

400 BCE
Giant Olmec sculptures in cities are smashed; archaeologists puzzled

1 CE to 750 CE
A huge city called Teotihuacán rises in Mexico; it has a

population between 125,000 and 200,000; one of the great cities of the world, it is destroyed around the year 750; archaeologists puzzled

December 31, 1999
In New York City a giant crystal ball was dropped; future archaeologists puzzled

Let me get this straight. We sleep on their beds. They feed us, and we don't even have to wag our tails. And people think they domesticated us???

and is used by humans. Cats and dogs are domesticated animals.

Corn is a great food for humans and animals. It's full of sugar, starches, and vitamins and grows fast in all sorts of conditions. It can sometimes survive on just a little water. Corn ground up into flour makes great tortillas; dried corn can last for a long time. Corn on the cob is fun to eat. *It's the only vegetable that you throw away the outside, cook the inside, eat the outside, and throw away the inside.* But corn just can't grow unless people put its seeds in the ground.

Farming: Hard Work That Can Make You Sick

All over the world, scientists are discovering that when people first became farmers, their teeth and bones show they were often sicker than the gatherers and hunters. Farming is very hard work. Ask anyone who farms (but don't expect a very long answer, because farmers are extremely busy people). The ancient farmers of Mexico and Peru probably had to work four to six days a week in the field. Meanwhile, ancient Americans in California and the Pacific Northwest probably spent only two or three days a week gathering plants and hunting. Children living in most gathering and hunting communities usually didn't have to work hard. Children in places where people farmed often worked in the field almost as soon as they learned to walk.

Even though it's hard work, farming means that people can stay in one place and know there's going to be food. Once people stay in one place, they almost always decide it's a great idea to build something, not just a place to live in, but something big and beautiful. The Olmecs, for example, were really into big — especially when it came to swelled heads. They carved some of the largest sculptures of human heads ever seen on Earth.

Where did I come from?

The stalk brought you.

Olmec: The Mother Culture

Some scholars call the Olmecs the "mother culture," because so many of the great empires in North America were built using the Olmec way of life as a foundation. Most archaeologists think the Olmecs were the first people in North America to construct pyramids and to invent what scholars believe were the beginnings of a writing system, a calendar, a counting system, and ball games.

Like most people, the Olmecs asked the great questions about birth, life, and death and tried to answer them. But because they left so many huge and beautiful artifacts, archaeologists know more about what the Olmecs thought than about most other ancient Americans who lived at the same time (and that's probably *exactly* how the Olmecs wanted it). Although many of the Olmec paintings and sculptures were destroyed or got covered up by the jungle, enough survived to help scholars and others appreciate their way of life.

Olmec Big Heads

Traces of the Olmec culture remained hidden for centuries because the jungles of Mexico and Central America swallowed up the Olmec cities. In 1862, plantation workers in Huaypan,

Veracruz, Mexico, found what looked like a huge kettle buried in the ground. Thinking there might be gold stashed inside, they started digging. What they uncovered wasn't a kettle after all. It was a sculpted helmet sitting atop a huge stone head.

Fifteen of these amazing heads have been found so far. They are thought to be sculptures of Olmec rulers. Each head is more than nine feet tall and weighs between 20 and 50 tons, about the size of a full-grown Stegosaurus dinosaur. It's mind-boggling to think of the work that went

into creating these gigantic monuments. Olmec artists carved the sculptures from basalt, a stone that came from mountains more than 40 miles away. Keep in mind that basalt is a very hard stone and the Olmecs didn't have metal tools, just tools made of stone, bone, or wood. The giant heads were probably partially carved at the quarry site and then dragged to rivers and loaded on very large rafts, which sounds a lot easier than it probably was.

Big Babies

The Olmecs were one of the few ancient civilizations anywhere to celebrate the human baby. They made life-size sculptures of babies, standing and crawling alone. Sculptures were sort of like the Olmec way of taking baby pictures, but the babies had to sit still for a *really* long time.

Archaeologists wonder if the babies are statues of gods or of royal children. The Olmecs also sculpted beautiful jade statues of babies that are part human and part jaguar. (Hopefully nobody modeled for those!) They may also have created sculptures showing what fetuses in the womb

Explanation for Stone Babies (artist's concept)

Happy birthday, honey! Hope you enjoy your stone baby!

Olmec sculptures have been collected by many museums. Examples can be seen in the **Museo Nacional de Antropología** in Mexico City, Mexico, the **Metropolitan Museum of Art** in New York City, and the **Brooklyn Museum of Art** in New York City.

would have looked like. Many art historians believe that Olmec sculptors are among the greatest artists not only of the ancient world but of all time.

You know, they've got half-lion people, half-eagle people, goat people, horse, fish, and snake people. How come you never see a half-roach person?

The Olmec Religion

Because so many Olmec stone monuments survived, archaeologists have searched for clues to their religion. At the same time that the Egyptians were building their pyramids, the Olmecs were also creating pyramids. They seem to have used the pyramids to watch the skies for omens about the future and to discover the best time to plant crops. They worshiped spirits of the sun, moon, and stars. The Olmecs believed all people traveled from a watery

76

Have a Heart

For years, most scholars were not sure that the Olmecs practiced human sacrifice to their gods. In 1997, a heart doctor and art historian found a 3,000-year-old anatomically correct ceramic human heart that an Olmec potter crafted. It's the oldest image of a heart in the world. The doctor who found it believes that it shows that the Olmecs would sometimes cut out a human heart and offer it to the gods as a sacrifice so that their crops would grow. Many of the cultures of Mexico and Central America that came after the Olmecs continued this practice.

I got a dead chicken and some snakes. What did you get?

Some frogs. Haven't these people ever heard of pizza?

Sacrifice, the practice of killing an animal or a human in order to try to please or send a message to a god, was practiced in many places in the ancient world. In the Bible, Abraham thought that his god wanted him to sacrifice his son, Isaac. Alexander the Great of ancient Greece never went into battle without whipping out his sword and plunging it into an animal like a horse.

underworld up to Earth, and then after death they continued on up to the sky. Many animals were also considered divine, especially the snake and the jaguar. One Olmec legend said that a woman and a jaguar mated and gave birth to a race of creatures that were half human, half animal.

Do they call Pacific Islanders Hula People? No.
Do they call the French people Eiffel Tower People? No.
Are people in the United States called Hamburger and French Fry People? Nope.
But we're stuck with the Rubber People forever!

The First Ball Games, or Anybody for a Game of "Sacrifice the Loser"?

The Olmecs built huge ceremonial ball courts for their games, something we still do today, only now we add retractable domes and luxury suites. Some of the sculptures sur- rounding Olmec ball courts suggest that they also may have paraded prisoners of war into the courts and sacrificed them there. Many other ancient cultures in the Americas copied Olmec ball courts and played different versions of their ball games.

The Olmecs were probably the first people to use sap or latex from rubber trees. They cured it over fire to make raincoats or rubber-coated ponchos. They made rubber-soled shoes for walking and rubber bottles to hold water. They also molded rubber into balls for their games. Actually, it was rubber that led to the name of these ancient people. The Aztec people, who came to power in Mexico nearly 25 centuries later, called their predecessors "Olmecs," which means rubber in Nahuatl, the Aztec language.

Beautiful Cities

Around 1200 BCE, the Olmecs established the great city the Spaniards later called San Lorenzo. A few hundred years later, the Olmecs founded the city called La Venta by the Spanish. With their many sculptures, ball courts, and

La Venta in Mexico is now a tropical outdoor museum near the Gulf of Mexico. There you can walk among the two dozen huge stone heads, altars, and strange half-human, half-jaguar figures.

pools of water (not to mention all that rubber stuff), San Lorenzo and La Venta must have been beautiful. The Olmecs built San Lorenzo high above the river and created a huge, 16-story mound in the city's center. Some archaeologists believe that the Olmecs laid out the entire city of San Lorenzo in the shape of a gigantic bird flying east. What a weird coincidence! Poverty Point was built only a few hundred years earlier, and it is also partially in the shape of a giant bird. Then, 3,000 years later, in 1782, Americans in the United States picked the eagle as their national bird.

Artist's Theory 49: What happened to the Olmec giant stone heads

Rock termites

Daniel, Daniel, Daniel! Where do you come up with this stuff? I'm a bug. I know bugs! There are no "Rock termites"!

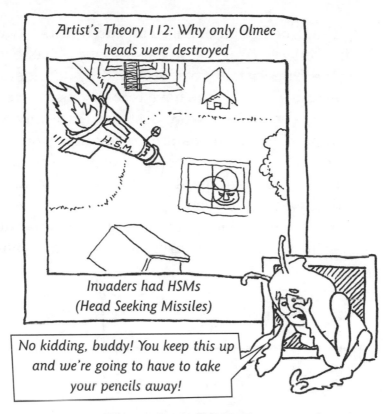

Artist's Theory 112: Why only Olmec heads were destroyed

Invaders had HSMs (Head Seeking Missiles)

No kidding, buddy! You keep this up and we're going to have to take your pencils away!

Smashed Heads

The great Olmec civilization lasted nearly 1,000 years, roughly as long as the golden age of Greece. Then, around 900 BCE, many of the Olmecs' colossal carved heads in San Lorenzo were smashed, leaving Olmecs with what can only be described as a colossal headache. Five hundred years later, in 400 BCE, the sculptures in La Venta were also destroyed. In both cities, the sculptures looked as if a giant kid stomped through a giant sand castle.

The destruction of the sculptures in the two main Olmec cities led archaeologists to believe that the Olmecs had been attacked by outsiders. However, archaeologists have recently discovered that only the statues were destroyed, not any of the Olmecs' homes or palaces. They now wonder if perhaps when an Olmec ruler died, his monuments were destroyed. It seems kind of selfish, but that's a king for you.

After archaeologists realized that the smashed Olmec sculptures didn't mean that

Artist's Theory 347:
Why did the Olmecs leave?

Stop it!

After years of inexplicable feelings that they were being watched, the Olmecs packed it in.

entire cities were destroyed, they were even more mystified as to why the Olmec empire declined.

Some archaeologists believe that the mystery goes back to those little ears of corn. The more the Olmecs depended upon corn as a crop, the more they planted the same fields again and again. (You'd think after 1,000 years, they'd get tired of corn dishes.) If land is farmed too much, too little grows on it. The Olmecs probably produced less and less corn, and without a strong food crop nearby, people probably moved away from the Olmec cities. Eventually, the jungle covered up the cities, and they stayed covered for centuries.

Teotihuacán: The Big Apple of the Ancient American World

Shortly after the fall of the Olmec Empire, around the date that on our calendar we would call the year 1 — the beginning of the Common Era — Teotihuacán, the greatest city in all of ancient America, grew up right in the middle of Mexico. Just 20 miles outside of present-day Mexico City, the ancient ruins of Teotihuacán are now nearly empty and are preserved as a world heritage site. Empty, that is, except for the tourists who come to stare at its massive pyramids, ball courts, and temples.

Amazingly, some attitudes of "big city" people have remained incredibly familiar over the years.

Yo! What are you lookin' at? You lookin' at me? Whadda ya got a problem?

During the first half of the first millennium, up to about the year 750, Teotihuacán had a population of perhaps 200,000. Archaeologists believe that the inhabitants of Teotihuacán thought their city was the center of the universe. (Lots of people accuse 21st-century New Yorkers of thinking the same thing.) Teotihuacán *was* one of the greatest cities of the ancient world and one of the most mysterious: Why and how did it become so huge? And who exactly built it, anyway?

Great cities are often also great trading centers, and Teotihuacán was probably no exception. Turquoise from as far away as Arizona and New Mexico found its way to the city. For food, Teotihuacánians depended on corn.

Strangely, for such a great city, nobody yet knows much about the people who created it. (Maybe its inhabitants didn't make enough things out of rubber.) The people of Teotihuacán almost never made statues of individual rulers the way the Olmecs did. Instead, their artwork was usually a tribute to their gods and goddesses. Many historians believe that there was never one great ruler, but that several families shared in the ruling of the city.

Until the 1960s, most scholars thought that Teotihuacán was a peaceful city. Then they discovered the bones of hundreds of human sacrifices and paintings of captives getting their hearts cut out. The place doesn't seem as peaceful anymore.

Anyone for a Walk Up the Avenue of the Dead?

Today in Teotihuacán, tourists stroll along an impressive main street. Seventy-five temples line this street; many of them contain the bones of hundreds of human sacrifices. (Sounds like a better place to race through than to stroll through.) Like New York City, the streets of Teotihuacán follow a block-by-block grid; picture Broadway — without all the taxis. A great north–south roadway runs the entire length of the city. When the Aztecs discovered the nearly empty city, they called this main street the Avenue of the

I left my heart in Teotihuacán . . .

Dead. The name stuck. And why not? After all, it's so catchy!

The Pyramid of the Moon marks the northern end of the avenue. Standing nearly 138 feet tall, it only looks small compared to the huge Pyramid of the Sun in the middle of the avenue. The Pyramid of the Sun is the biggest pyramid in the world, rising to a height of more than 200 feet. It is far bigger than the Egyptian pyramids. Underneath the pyramid is a long cave.

Do you believe this, honey? We build a giant pyramid and the Sun family has to build a bigger one, right down the street!

Moon family

Teotihuacán in Mexico. Only 20 miles outside of Mexico City, the ruins of Teotihuacán are one of the most frequently visited ancient sites in the Americas. You can walk the Avenue of the Dead, and if you're not afraid of heights, probably climb the Pyramids of the Sun and Moon.

Archaeologists think this cave was the most sacred place in the whole city, the place where the goddess of corn was thought to have lived.

A Great City Empties

People began moving away from Teotihuacán by about the year 700. The skeletons of the people who lived in the city show that they were sick a lot. In 750, the center of the city was destroyed by fire. The pyramids survived, but almost nobody lived there anymore. Despite many sacrifices to the gods, the land around Teotihuacán wasn't able to support its huge population. The great city emptied.

I only have one thing to say about those ancient Americans — corn! Sure, they were amazing artists who built an extraordinary city with enormous pyramids, but let me tell you, nothing thrills this roach like a few buttery pieces of popcorn dropped on the movie-house floor. Thank you, Olmecs!

Those ancient Americans loved their corn! And not in the way that you "love" the color blue, then change your mind a week later and decide you now "love" the color red. I mean those people couldn't live without that crop. They had corn gods, they sacrificed other humans so their corn would grow better, and when they ran out of corn, what did they do? They moved away!

Now *that's* love.

Anyway, while the Olmecs were busy pulling their ears, other ancient Americans farther north found something to do with their land besides farm it. . . . And they didn't even need corn *or* corny jokes.

Chapter 5

Here a Mound, There a Mound...

Around the same time that the people of Teotihuacán were farming corn and building their great city, far north in what is now Ohio ancient Americans were creating spectacular earthen sculptures. Earth building didn't just go on in Ohio. Archaeologists now believe there were actually several different groups of ancient Americans who built mounds at different times. But nobody knows exactly why or even who these people were. Some people think that the mounds might have been built by aliens from outer space

TIME LINE

Around 700 to 100 BCE
Adena people of Ohio create earthworks and elaborate burial grounds

Around 100 BCE to 600 CE
Hopewell people of Ohio make mysterious circles and squares out of earth; most of these circles

and squares are not used for burials

as landing spots for their spaceships. Almost all archaeologists do not believe the mounds have anything to do with spaceships, but they really are not  sure why people went on such a mound-building spree. There are thousands of them, discovered all over the Midwest and the East of what is now the United States. That hill in your own backyard could be the remains of one of America's mounds.

Mound Builder, Mound Builder, Build Me a Mound

Because nobody knows what the Mound Builders called themselves, archaeologists, as usual, named them for the place where mounds were first found. The oldest Ohio Mound Builders

1077
The Serpent's Mound of Ohio is constructed

Around 600 to 1300
Ancient Americans in Wisconsin, Iowa, and Minnesota build effigy mounds in the shape of lizards, huge birds, and marching bears; almost none of them are used for burials

1301
After playing in the dirt for thousands of years, ancient Americans begin the enormous task of doing their laundry

are the Adena people, named after Adena Plantation, the Ohio farm where the mounds were discovered in the 19th century.

The Adena cone-shaped mounds are full of human remains, mostly ones burned in a funeral pyre. So far at least 500 Adena mounds have been discovered in Ohio, Kentucky, Indiana, and Pennsylvania. (Adena burial sites that aren't mounds have also been found from New York to the Chesapeake Bay.) Whoever the Adena people were, they went to great trouble when it came time to bury a relative. Archaeologists think they have figured out the steps the Adena went through. It was as complicated a process as what the Egyptians went through to create their mummies.

all this talk about mounds... REALLY made me want a candy bar. Went to the store. Back in a minute
Mel

First, the Adena would place the person's remains outdoors so that vultures could pick the bones clean. Then, they would burn the bones and cover them with red paint. After the remains of the dead were prepared, the Adena buried them with many artifacts. In one case, they even took down a house and buried it with the person. Elaborately carved pipes, stone tools, and clay pots have been found alongside Adena remains. Some people were buried with sheets of hammered copper, occasionally designed in the shape of a bird in flight.

I guess he decided he could take it with him.

In most Adena burial mounds, everyone seems to have gotten a share of the wealth. Archaeologists wonder if the Adena people were making a point that in their society, people were treated equally. Or were the Adena only treated equally when they were dead? Or maybe they were saying you really *can* take it with you.

Grave Creek Mound State Park in Moundsville, West Virginia, has an Adena mound surrounded by a moat. Many objects found in the burial mound are in the museum. The **Ohio Historical Center** in Columbus, Ohio, has a great collection of burial items from Adena graves.

The Hopewell:
The Spectacular Geometry Folks

For a brief period, it seemed as if the ancient Americans stopped building mounds. Then from around 100 BCE to 600 CE, the people who lived in and around Ohio went on another mound-building spree. These Mound Builders are called the Hopewell people, after Mordecai Hopewell, a 19th-century farmer who found 30 mounds on his farm.

The Hopewell Mound Builders constructed curious squares and circles that were perfectly geometrical. It was as if a giant math teacher reached

Darn gophers!

think it was a foundation for a supermarket.

I think it was a big, flat, one-story pyramid.

Maybe they were really afraid of floods.

Or they were having a really big party and needed a really big table.

Maybe the square is natural, and the rest of the U.S. just eroded away.

STUMP THE ARCHAEOLOGISTS!

down and used the dirt of Ohio to teach shapes. One mound forms a perfect square so gigantic that more than 100 baseball diamonds could fit inside it. The Hopewell buried very few bodies in these mounds. So the real stumper for historians is: Why were the Hopewell people mound builders?

Archaeologists think that the Hopewell mounds were built for a religious purpose. But what was the Hopewell people's religion? Scientists don't know for sure, but they believe that it spread from people to people, the same way Christianity and Buddhism spread, until there were worshipers over a wide area.

Recently, archaeologists have discovered traces of what they call the Great Hopewell Road. Think of it as Ohio's first highway. This road seems to have connected two different sets of mounds 60 miles apart. The road may have been used by worshipers gathering for religious

Looks like they're piling dirt up for us now.

I wish they'd just sacrifice a pizza.

ceremonies. The mounds might have been a way for ancient Americans to celebrate the way Earth was created and to honor their gods for creating the world.

One of the weirdest Hopewell mounds is actually one of the smaller ones. It's called the "mound of pipes," because there are more than 250 beautiful pipes buried in this mound. The pipes are carved in the shapes of animals, birds, and reptiles. No one is sure exactly what the Hopewell smoked in these pipes, but archaeologists think the pipes were probably used by shamans, or spiritual guides, for religious ceremonies. The Hopewell people left no written records (which is so like early humans), so all archaeologists have to go on are the artifacts they find buried in mounds.

One thing artifacts do show is that the Hopewell people probably were great traders.

The Hopewell used seashells in their jewelry and pearls on their beautiful handwoven robes. These objects must have come from trading with people as far away as the Atlantic Ocean near Florida, probably people who needed pipes. The Hopewell also wore copper headdresses shaped like deer antlers; the copper came from upper Michigan. They even collected alligator teeth and barracuda jaws that they must have gotten through trading with people from the Gulf of Mexico area. Some Hopewell bodies were buried with thousands of shimmering pieces of mica from North Carolina. Each mica piece was carefully carved in the shape of a bird and sometimes a human hand. The mica pieces had tiny holes in them, so they could be sewn onto clothing like spangles. The more archaeologists study ancient Americans, the more they realize how much they seem to have traded with one another.

At **Hopewell Culture National Park** in Chillicothe, Ohio, you can climb onto an observation deck to get a good view of the mounds. At **Moundbuilders State Memorial** in Newark, Ohio, you can see an earthwork 1,200 feet across. Its walls are from 8 to 14 feet tall.

Lizards and Birds and Bears . . . Oh, My!

Slightly farther west of Ohio, in areas of what is now Wisconsin, Iowa, and Minnesota, another group of ancient Americans also built huge earthworks between the years 600 and 1300. These people are called the Effigy people because they made their mounds into effigies or shapes of living creatures such as lizards, bears, birds, and people. One human figure is 125 feet long; that's about as long as a 12-story building lying on its side. One of the Effigy people's most amazing earthen sculptures is in the shape of six giant marching bears. One great bear mound would put Godzilla to shame — it's almost 70 feet across at the shoulders!

The Effigy people almost never buried their dead in these mounds. Some archaeologists believe that the earthwork animals might be symbols of different tribes or clans. If you were coming to a big celebration and were part of the bear clan, you'd see the giant bear mounds and know where to go. Other

98

scientists think that the mounds were one way that ancient Americans kept track of the celestial movements of the sun, moon, planets, and stars. Effigy mounds are yet another mystery about the ancient Americans just waiting to be solved.

The Mound That Looks Like a Snake

Ancient America's great masterpiece of an earthen sculpture is found in Ohio and is built in

Effigy Mounds National Monument in Marquette, Iowa. The marching bears, birds, and other mounds can be seen for miles along the cliffs where the Yellow River meets the Mississippi.

the shape of a snake. It's 1,254 feet long (more than four football fields). The snake's head rests on a cliff overlooking a small river. This head has a huge, perfect oval on it. Is it an egg in the snake's mouth? Is it the snake's eye? Who can say? Nobody knows exactly why early Americans built the snake or what the egg is, or even if it is an egg.

The people who built Serpent Mound did not bury anything in it. With no burial artifacts, archaeologists couldn't do radiocarbon dating. So, for many years, most scientists thought Serpent Mound was about 2,000 years old. Then in 1991, archaeologists discovered some tiny charcoal samples in the mound. Using the most

Well, nobody can accuse him of hiding like a snake in the grass.

Serpent Mound in Locust Grove, Ohio, about 100 miles south of Columbus in south-central Ohio. There is a museum on the grounds that shows exhibits on the mound and how it might have been made.

sophisticated radiocarbon dating tools, they were able to date Serpent Mound. They found it was not as old as they first thought. Serpent Mound was probably built in 1070. In 1054, Halley's Comet blazed very close to Earth. Scholars now wonder whether the serpent really represents a comet's tail. Serpent Mound is the first prehistoric site that was declared a national monument in the United States.

With all those mysteries and still no written records, it's no wonder that North America's ancient history drives scholars bonkers. But there was one ancient civilization in North America that left more than hints about themselves. These ancient Americans wrote their history down. The trouble was that nobody could read it until almost the end of the 20th century!

Look at me! I'm King of the Hill! Or is it King of the Mound? This isn't just a pile of dirt I'm standing on. Well, technically it is, but it's also much more. It's a place of worship; it's a kind of cemetery. Of course, an ancient mound of

dirt is much harder to interpret than an ancient inscription. That's why historians love the next group of people to come along. When it came to their story, they put it in writing! I like them, too. They invented chocolate.

Chapter 6
Maya Can Build Better

The Maya were the first people in the Americas who recorded their history in books. They also invented one of the world's most accurate and sophisticated counting systems; they waged wars, practiced human sacrifice, and farmed the land around their cities until almost nothing grew. Empires have a way of doing that: They are great in wonderful ways, but also great in horrible ways.

If you think of a great civilization as having imperial kings and queens and incredible cities

TIME LINE

August 12, 1114 BCE
Beginning of the world, according to the Maya

219 CE
Founding of the dynasty at Tikal, one of the great Maya city-states, during the reign of Yax-Moch Xok

603
King Pakal the Great born at Palenque

104

So does this make your average Maya a sort of farmer–warrior–accountant?

filled with pyramids and temples painted inside and out with gorgeous red and blue murals, then the Maya were probably the greatest ancient civilization in North America.

Maya royal families ruled from almost the year 1 CE until the Spanish arrived in the 1500s. At its height, the population of the Maya empire was probably between 12 million and 16 million people. There are still millions of people alive today who trace their history back to the ancient Maya and who speak their ancient language.

800 to 900	December 23, 2012	December 24, 2012
Maya cities in Guatemala and lowlands decline, but cities in Mexico gain power	End of the world, according to the ancient Maya calendar	Day we realize the world didn't end as the Maya expected . . . maybe!

The Maya were never united under one emperor. They lived in city-states, and scholars are still trying to figure out exactly how these cities were connected. Royal families ruled the cities, and there were often wars between the city-states. Sometimes royal families called a truce by arranging marriages among themselves.

Maya Writing Pioneers

Very few ancient civilizations anywhere in the world invented a written way to record their histories. In fact, scholars think that perhaps only a few groups in the Middle East and in Central America invented writing from scratch. The Maya were among these few. All other peoples of the world either got along by singing or reciting their history and legends or they borrowed writing from other cultures.

Breaking the Maya Code

The ancient Maya wrote in a mixed system of glyphs, or pictures (like the Egyptian hieroglyphics), and symbols for sounds (like the letters in this book). Maya glyphs were very hard for modern scholars to decipher. In fact, until the 1950s, nobody could read Maya writing.

Chocolate

Marriages were celebrated with a sacred chocolate drink, something that Maya people often still do today. Archaeologists believe that the Maya were the first to not only use chocolate but to possibly include it in spiritual ceremonies. (Maybe you have something in common with the Maya here?) A thousand-year-old vessel was found with traces of chocolate in it. Chocolate was probably eaten only by the wealthy. The Maya used chocolate in lots of different ways, including mixing it with honey and vanilla.

Okay, it's thousand-year-old chocolate, but it's still chocolate!

I can't make heads or tails out of this.

I think it actually is heads and tails.

Archaeologists now realize that Maya scribes were talented artists from royal families who often signed their work. There were special schools for Maya scribes who made beautiful accordion-folded books out of animal hide and tree bark.

When the Spanish invaded Maya territory in the 1500s, Spanish priests burned almost all the Maya books. A few Catholic priests managed to rescue four books out of what must have been thousands. Those four are the only Maya books that exist today. Lucky for us, the Maya also

Don't you just hate when they spring open like that?

carved their stories on almost all of their public buildings and artwork. The stone writing survived, but just like the books, no one could read the glyphs.

One of the many breakthroughs in Maya hieroglyphics happened in 1952. Archaeologists climbed to the top of one of the pyramids in the great Maya city of Palenque, near the Gulf Coast of southern Mexico. On their way down into the center of the pyramid, they found a passageway to a tomb that hadn't been opened in 1,200 years.

Using all available knowledge of Maya writing, the archaeologists were able to read many

How Scientists Finally Deciphered the
Maya Hieroglyphs in 1952

If I had been a king at 12, I would have made everybody dress up as superheroes!

inscriptions on the tomb. That's when they knew for sure that the Maya had monarchs. The tomb belonged to a Maya king named Pakal who had ruled from the time he was 12 until he was 80.

King Pakal died in the year 683. He was buried like an Egyptian pharaoh, with a jade mask on his face, hundreds of pearls, and other jade treasures. Several soldiers and servants were sacrificed and entombed with him. Being sacrificed and buried with a king was considered an honor.

Scholars who studied the Maya culture were particularly interested in the inscriptions on King Pakal's shield because it was so similar to the writing in the Maya books rescued by Spanish priests. Because those books had also been translated into Spanish, archaeologists were able to break the Maya code. When they did, they found out that

No, no, no! Don't get me wrong. The whole protecting the dead thing sounds great! It's the me being dead, too, part of it that I'm having trouble with.

the Maya inscriptions on Pakal's shield and on many of the monuments in Palenque told the story of the royal dynasty. It seems that the Maya

Of course I wrote about the royal dynasty. I was royal, too. Besides, what did you think this was? A diet book?

monarchs mostly wanted their priests and scribes to write about how great they were.

The more archaeologists learned about King Pakal, the more they realized he was a great leader. Like Elizabeth I of England, Pakal led a very long life. Though he was a warrior in his youth, when he was about 40, he became more and more interested in the arts. Again, like Queen Elizabeth I, who hired Shakespeare to write plays for her, King Pakal brought many of the finest Maya artists into his court and gave them work creating monuments to him.

Royal Life: It's Not All Fun and Games — It's Also a Lot of Ouch!

One of the duties of the Maya royal family was to offer blood to the gods so that the crops would grow. High-born queens pricked blood from their tongues, ears, or lips. High-born kings like Pakal had an even more painful ritual to

endure: putting thorns through their private parts. Ouch!

The Maya believed that their gods didn't just want a little blood. Most demanded human sacrifice, too. Without proper sacrifice, the Maya feared the rain would not fall, the sun would not shine, crops would not grow, and that basically everything would just collapse. Most of those sacrificed were captives from wars between the city-states. When the Maya fought wars, they tried to capture alive as many enemies as possible. The warriors and sons of enemy royal families were particularly prized. The captives were bound and brought back to the victorious city-state and sacrificed in elaborate ceremonies.

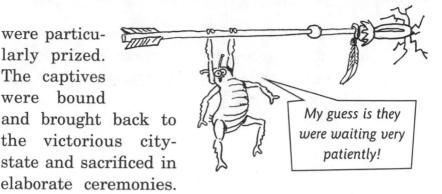

My guess is they were waiting very patiently!

The Maya kept records of these ceremonies in beautifully painted murals. In the murals at Bonampak, near the border between Mexico and Guatemala, the Maya ruler stands proudly in his jaguar-pelt jacket. Nearly naked prisoners cower below him, some already beheaded, others clearly waiting to be sacrificed.

Why the Gods Demanded Blood

There is still a lot of debate about exactly how much sacrificing went on in the Maya culture. For example, archaeologists once thought that at Chitzén Itzá, one of the last great Maya cities in Mexico, victims were bound and thrown down into deep wells. There's only one problem with this theory: When archaeologists emptied a well, they only found the bodies of a few old people. These old people might have drowned by accident.

However, there is very little doubt that the Maya used human sacrifice as part of their religion and to mark great occasions of state. Most of the bloodletting, both human sacrifices and royal donations of blood, was to make sure that the corn crops grew. After all, to the Maya, corn was the foundation of life.

Historians know more about the Maya religion than they do about most ancient American religions before the year 1000. Much of this information at first came from the *Popul Vuh*, the Maya book of creation that was translated into Spanish by a monk in the 1500s.

According to the *Popul Vuh*, the mythical

Next we'll meet He-Who-Farts himself! Get your cameras ready, we won't be slowing down. Okay, take a deep breath and hold it! Here we go!

Why the Maya Underworld Is Not One of the Great Tourist Attractions of the World:
- *The Maya word for devil is literally "one who farts."*
- *People in the underworld often wore necklaces of plucked eyeballs.*
- *Nobles of the Underworld included: Lord Scab-Stripper; Lord Blood Gatherer; Lord Demon of Pus; Lord Demon of Jaundice (and the somewhat less threatening Lord Milk-Through-Your-Nose). Okay, we made that last one up, but the rest of them were denizens of the Maya underworld.*

hero twins Hunahpu and Xbalanque went to the underworld to rescue their father the corn god and to bring corn back to the Maya people.

The Maya underworld was a very nasty place. Then again, with all those sacrifices going on, their regular world could be pretty grim, too. The hero twins had to wade through underworld rivers of blood and pus, but eventually they saved their father, their uncle, and the corn plant. The hero twins were also great musicians, dancers, and tricksters. They had lots of other adventures, many of them involving ball games. Hunahpu and Xbalanque were great ballplayers!

To celebrate the victory of the hero twins over the gods of the underworld, the Maya played ball games that acted out Hunahpu and Xbalanque's heroic escapades. These ball games were often the center of Maya public life. Festivals staged around the ball games included dancing, music, gambling, and an awful lot of feasting and partying.

Unlike the Olmec games, much more is known about how the Maya played their ball games. There were two teams of maybe two to three players; sometimes the game was even played one-on-one. The players wore heavy pads and had to strike a hard rubber ball with their bodies without using their hands or arms, just like in today's soccer. To win, a player had to kick or push the ball through a ring.

Foul! Hands! He touched the ball with his hands!

On special occasions, the Maya ball game was a real game of sudden death. Some of the paintings and sculptures around Maya ball courts show a ballplayer with his head cut off (guess he was the player who lost!) and blood streaming from his neck in the form of snakes, a symbol of fertile land. Sometimes the loser's head was wrapped in rubber and used as a ball in the next game.

What's Your Sign?

Foul! Uneccessary roughness . . . and I don't think a penalty kick is going to help.

The quality of everyday Maya life depended, of course, on whether you were part of the royal family, a priest, a warrior, a farmer, or a worker. (Of course, if you were a prisoner, everyday life was absolutely horrible, but at least it didn't last long!)

Scribes only wrote about the rulers, so it's hard to know what everyone else was doing. However, archaeologists continue to research

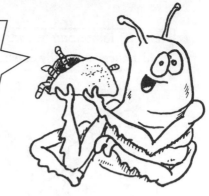

To me, just about anything sounds pretty yummy on a tortilla. Of course I am a cockroach, so just about anything on anything sounds yummy!

what everyday ancient Maya life might have been like. They have discovered that almost every Maya home had a fireplace with three stones to honor the families' ancestors. You'll still find this in many traditional Maya homes today.

The fireplace was used to cook tortillas, which the Maya made out of ground corn. (They are still made that way.) The Maya added tomatoes, chili peppers, and avocado to their tasty tortillas. Other Maya foods might not seem like such a taste treat to you. The Maya also ate dogs and bugs.

Much of everyone's life, even in the city-states, revolved around the planting season and especially the sowing of corn. Maya life was governed by feast days celebrating the different stages of the planting life and determined by their incredible calendar. The Maya were the most accurate timekeepers in the ancient world. They calculated the exact length of a year as 365.2422 days — they were off by less than .0007.

The Maya also had a sacred calendar that lasted 260 days, or nine months, almost the exact time that a woman is usually pregnant. Only

priests trained in Maya astrology could read this sacred calendar. It was used to foretell the future and avoid bad luck. If a child was born on an unlucky day, his or her naming ceremony would be put off until a luckier day. The Maya also had their own astrological zodiac of constellations. Scorpio, the sign of the scorpion, appears in the zodiac that we use today and in the Maya zodiac.

Maya Number System

The Maya are considered mathematical wizards. They used a system of dots and dashes; a simple drawing of a shell represented zero (there's an example on the next page). The Maya even developed the concept of zero, as did the Arabs in the Middle East.

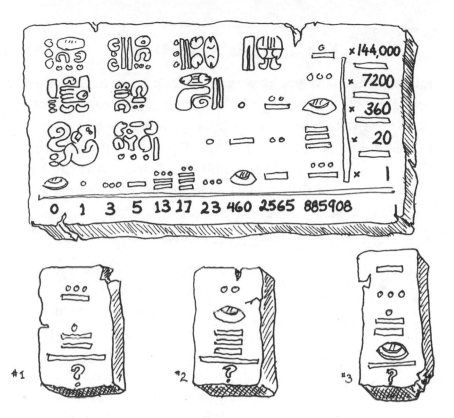

What Happened to the Maya?

After the year 800, many Maya moved north. They built cities such as Chitzén Itzá, and trading became even more important. Other Maya took to the sea. Like the Olmecs, the longer the Maya empire lasted, the more Maya farmers tried to harvest bigger and bigger amounts of corn. With this overuse, the fields became less

#1 172 #2 725 #3 57820

The Toltecs Take Over

Much of the Maya empire was eventually taken over by the Toltec people. According to the Aztecs (who came along later), the Toltecs were ruled by a wise, peace-loving king named Topiltzin Quetzacoatl who hated human sacrifice. Quetzacoatl was forced to flee his city. Some myths say he set sail across the Gulf of Mexico on a raft made of serpents, promising to someday return and claim his kingdom.

The Maya aren't the only guys who can use shells in their math. Punch in 77345 and then turn your calculator upside down.

fertile, and with corn scarce, the cities became crowded. Maya rulers and warriors fought wars for greater territory, but that probably ended up ruining even more farmland.

Some of the great cities like Palenque declined, but the Maya didn't die out. Much of their way of life — the ball games, pyramid building, and especially corn cultivation — moved north through Mexico and into what is now the United States.

There are many Maya sites that can be visited in Mexico, Guatemala, Belize, Honduras, and El Salvador. Here are just a few:

Palenque, Mexico You can see the original tomb of King Pakal. In 1998, another tomb containing the body of a queen was found. She also was wearing a jade mask.

Tikal, Guatemala This is often called the greatest of Guatemala's 3,000 Maya sites. Twin pyramids face each other across a vast plaza. At the Pyramid of the Giant Jaguar is the tomb of some of the mightiest Maya rulers. Tikal is part of a national park, and there are a beautiful rain forest and lots of wild animals to see, too.

Chitzén Itzá is near Cancún, Mexico. You can climb a nine-story pyramid and picture yourself being sacrificed on top of it. (You may feel like being sacrificed after the climb!) Do not try this if you are afraid of heights. You can also see a 500-foot-long ball court.

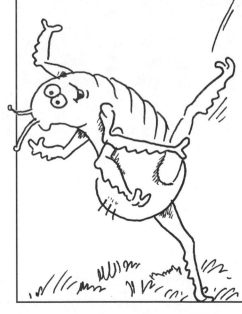

Those ancient Maya sure were confusing people. They invented their own system of writing and that's good. But they pulled people's hearts out and that's bad. They built amazing pyramids and painted stunning murals and that's good. But they tied people to stakes and shot arrows at them and that's bad. They were able to figure out almost exactly how many days were in a year and that's good. But they played soccer with a dead guy's head and that's bad. At least, it sure sounds bad. I guess it just goes to show that nobody's perfect. But the bottom line is that no matter what they did wrong, no matter who they shot arrows at, no matter whose head they played soccer with, the ancient Maya loved chocolate and that can only mean one thing — they were my kind of people!

But the Maya weren't the only game in town; there were other people around at the same time — and they also did some pretty amazing stuff themselves. . . .

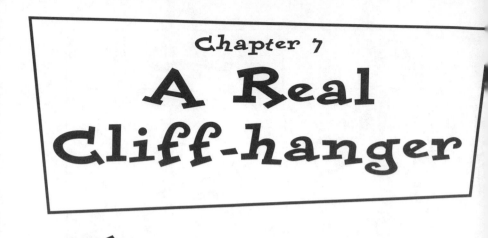

Chapter 7
A Real Cliff-hanger

The first people to farm corn in what is now the United States lived in Arizona, near the Mexican border. These ancient Americans couldn't have picked a more difficult place to farm. The Southwest desert is dry. It's hot. It's got rattlesnakes and scorpions. So why would anybody want to farm there?

Some hints:

- The Southwest desert is close to Mexico, so people could have easily learned about planting corn by trading with the people of Teotihuacán and the Maya.

TIME LINE

300 *to* 1000
The Hohokam people farm and build cities in Arizona

900 *to* 1100
The Anasazi ancestors of the Pueblo people build multi-room dwellings in cliffs

1882–2000
Multiroom dwellings are built in New York City; roaches move in

124

- The desert isn't *completely* dry. In the spring, snow melts in the mountains, and streams overflow their banks. In the summer, great thunderstorms explode over the mountains. There are even rivers in the desert.

- The ancient Americans were hardy, stubborn, and persistent. At one time, they had lived in the southwestern desert and hunted mammoths. When the mammoths died out, they hunted bison. When the bison moved to richer grassland in the North, some people stayed put in the desert. Apparently just like today, people liked to live and play in places like Phoenix, Arizona.

Starting around the year 500, Phoenix became the site of one of the largest cities in ancient America. It was home to the Hohokam people. The Hohokam people were incredibly ambitious when it came to farming in the desert. They didn't let a

Sure! It rains in the desert, but it can really be quite localized!

little thing like almost no water stop them. They built nearly *1,000 miles* of irrigation canals in and around present-day Phoenix.

Nothing's more romantic than the famous canals of Phoenix.

Some archaeologists think the Hohokam people originally were exiles from the great empires of Mexico.

Clues that the Hohokam might have come from Mexico:

- They built huge ball courts.
- They built their cities around a central plaza.
- They grew corn.

Clues that the Hohokam might *not* have been Maya:

- They built very different ball courts from those the Maya built.

- They had no written language.
- It doesn't look like they practiced human sacrifice.

Play Ball!

Ball games were almost an obsession with the Hohokam (and this was way before ESPN!). They had a network of more than 200 ball courts. Some of them were huge. There are still the remains of an ancient ball court beneath what is now downtown Phoenix. This one is more than 200 feet long, longer than two football fields.

The Phoenix ball court is so big that archaeologists think the Hohokam played a different game than the Maya. In the Maya games, there were usually only one or two people on a team. The Hohokam games probably had much bigger

Hey, Dad! Is the ball game almost on?

Great! Want some popcorn?

Yep! It's coming right up in about 1,500 years.

teams, more like modern soccer. Of course, since nobody seems to have gotten killed for losing, it was much easier to find players.

Scientists are looking for clues about the Hohokam in the thousands of clay human figures that these ancient people left behind, although most of those were found smashed. Archaeologists are piecing together those clay statues. They think the figures will provide information as to how the Hohokam people lived. They may also learn more about whether the Hohokam were Maya, Olmecs, Toltecs, or whether they were people from Teotihuacán who came north, or descendants of Clovis and Folsom people who had never left their homeland.

Chaco Canyon: A Strange Place in More Ways than One

One of the most unusual towns in ancient America was built directly into a cliff and along the valley floor of a deep canyon. This town is in Chaco Canyon, New Mexico. Some archaeologists have compared it to the Emerald City of Oz (except there was no wizard and the horses didn't change colors). Chaco Canyon seems like a strange place to build a city. It only gets nine inches of rain a year. It's now mostly a wilderness of saltbush, snakeweed, prickly pears, mice, lizards, and an occasional rattlesnake. On ter-

At the **Casa Grande Ruins National Monument** in Coolidge, Arizona, just east of Phoenix, you can see a Hohokam "big" house, several stories high. **Arizona State University Museum of Anthropology** in Tempe, Arizona, and the **Pueblo Grande Museum** in Phoenix have extensive exhibits on life during both the prehistoric and historic periods.

races above the river, the ancestral Puebloans (Anasazi) planted corn and built great plazas and tall buildings. The greatest building in Chaco Canyon is called Pueblo Bonito (beautiful town). Pueblo Bonito is about four or five stories high and is twice as long and twice as wide as a football field. It took more than a million cut-and-fitted bricks to build. Giant tree trunks were used as beams to hold up the walls. Some of these wooden beams weighed as much as 600 pounds. Pueblo Bonito has nearly 800 rooms. Until 1882, when an apartment house went up in New York City, Pueblo Bonito had more rooms than any other building in American history.

Archaeologists used to think that every room in Pueblo Bonito held a family. Then they realized that there were almost no traces of grains, fruits and vegetables, animal bones, or ash and charcoal in Pueblo Bonito. These are all things that would have proved that families lived in the rooms (and didn't clean up after themselves!). Instead, archaeologists found signs of wealth, such as arrowheads made of valuable obsidian and carved frogs inlaid with turquoise. Turquoise was as valuable as gold in the Southwest and Mexico 1,000 years ago. The brilliant blue stone is still used in jewelry created by the Pueblo people today.

The Anasazi and How They Got Their Name

One of the best-known ancient American groups of the Southwest has been called the Anasazi. Anasazi means "ancient enemies" in the language of the Navajo people who settled in the Southwest after the Anasazi. Navajo itself comes from a Spanish word that means "enemy of plowed fields."

Pueblo is the Spanish word for village. It also became the name for the many different peoples the Spanish encountered when they reached the Southwest. Today, many descendants of these ancient American people call themselves the Pueblo people. Pueblo people prefer that the Anasazi be called "the ancestors of the Pueblo people" or "ancestral Puebloans" in history books. The Navajo also now prefer to be called the Dine, their own name for themselves.

Signs of such wealth have changed how archaeologists look at the people of Chaco Canyon. Some of them now believe that perhaps the people of Chaco Canyon were very powerful warriors. The rooms of Pueblo Bonito might have been used to store tribute that they won in wars. Near Chaco Canyon, archaeologists have found pits filled with burned and broken human bones. In one pit they found the fractured skulls and smashed jaws of 470 men, women, and children. This has reinforced the idea that the people of Chaco Canyon were not as peaceful as everyone once thought. (You could call this a "dead give-away.") Other archaeologists believe that the

You can see the ruins of Pueblo Bonito at **Chaco Culture National Historical Park** in northwestern New Mexico. **Mesa Verde National Park** in southwestern Colorado is considered one of the most important archaeological sites in the world. There are several hikes to look at ruins along the cliff edge. Neither site is recommended for anyone who's afraid of heights.

Chaco Canyon people themselves were attacked by warriors from Mexico.

There is further evidence that Chaco Canyon might have been the hub of something like an empire. Archaeologists have uncovered more than 400 miles of straight roads leading out of the canyon. These roads lay hidden for centuries, covered over by desert sand, until the twentieth century, when road outlines showed up in infrared aerial photographs.

Excuse me. Do you know how to get to Chaco Canyon?

Sure. See all these straight roads? Take one.

Many scientists believe the roads were used by ancestral Puebloans to travel to and from religious ceremonies in Chaco Canyon. Throughout the canyon, there are many sacred underground pits that the modern Hopi, Zuni, and other Pueblo peoples call kivas. The Pueblo people believe that life is a journey from the underground world of darkness up into the light. The ceremonial kivas symbolize this belief: The only way in or out of a kiva is through a hole in the roof. If you visit Chaco Canyon, you can climb into the ancient kivas.

Around the year 1130, rain stopped falling around Chaco Canyon and did not return in any normal pattern for 50 years. This was not only bad news for the corn crops, it probably also put a few Pueblo weatherpeople out of work. Another large town was built farther north in Mesa Verde, Colorado. Chaco Canyon became practically a ghost town. By the time of this drought, corn farming had made its way east to the Mississippi River — and another great city was about to become the new ancient Emerald City!

And the Chaco Canyon forecast? We are in soooo much trouble. And tomorrow? We'll still be in trouble.

You know, when I was a young cockroach, I used to sleep in a bunk bed that had a ladder, but it was nothing like this! What if you were afraid of heights? What if you wanted to get a pizza delivered? What if you had to go to the bathroom in the middle of the night?

It sure is cool up here, though. I can even see every one of the ball courts, which means I could have watched all 200 games from the comfort of my own home. This is way better than ESPN! I'd never have to leave my house. It's a good thing, too, because I wouldn't know how to get out of here even if I wanted to.

It's hard to think of a more impressive place than Pueblo Bonito, but you know those humans: Bigger is always better. Wait till you see St. Louis . . . well, what eventually became St. Louis.

Chapter 8

C-A-H-O-
K-I-A!
OK!

By around the year 700, people along the Mississippi, Ohio, and some eastern rivers were planting corn. They began living in towns. Around the year 1000, there was an impressive city called Cahokia right in the middle of the United States. Cahokia had started out as just one of a string of tiny Mississippi River towns, but once the Cahokians started building, they just didn't stop. Most archaeologists believe Cahokia was larger than London or Paris at the time.

Cahokia was the name that people from the

TIME LINE

700
People start to build a giant pyramid in Cahokia, near what is now St. Louis, Missouri; archaeologists do not know exactly who does this or why

Around 800
Corn is planted by people east of the Mississippi; the Woodland people hunt with bows and arrows instead of spears

Around 900
East of the Mississippi River, more people live in villages and trade with one another; the village of Cahokia grows

136

Illini tribe gave to this great mysterious city after it was already almost empty. Today the city's ruins lie in the suburb of the same name, right across the Mississippi River from St. Louis, Missouri.

By the year 1000, archaeologists think that some 30,000 people may have called Cahokia home. Who were these people? Some believe that they might have been ancient Toltec or Maya people escaping from the wars in the Mexican

1000
Cahokia goes through a sudden growth spurt and becomes the biggest and most powerful city within what is now the United States

1100
Cahokia is under attack and defends itself

1965
Americans build a giant golden arch over St. Louis; future archaeologists believe it had to something to do with the worship of hamburgers

Yucatán around the island of Cancún. They could have come up the Mississippi River. Others believe that the Cahokians were ancestors of some of the first woodland gatherers and hunters who settled along the Mississippi River after the ice age.

Whoever they were, archaeologists have discovered that around the year 1000 Cahokia grew by leaps and bounds. It became much bigger than any other town along the Mississippi River. Small neighborhood courtyards vanished. A huge plaza was built in front of a pyramid that hadn't been there before.

Cahokia's Great Pyramid

The most impressive structure in Cahokia is a giant pyramid called Monk's Mound. It's called that because Catholic priests later built on it, not

The Possible Beginnings of the Great City of Cahokia

Hey! Is anybody else here tired of living in the forest?

because it belonged to a guy named Monk. Archaeologists are not sure why the people of Cahokia built such a huge pyramid.

Why do humans always measure everything by how many football fields fit inside it?

The Cahokia pyramid was built in stages over at least three centuries. Its base is larger than any in Egypt. The pyramid has four terraces and today, after nearly 1,000 years of erosion, is still more than 90 feet tall. Its base is 14 acres wide. Twelve football fields would fit inside it.

The Cahokians created Monk's Mound by carrying baskets of earth by hand. They moved 22 million cubic feet of dirt! No wonder it took more than 300 years to make it! This pyramid is the biggest monument in Cahokia, but there are

"River view! River view!" That's what the realtor kept saying. Now look out there! Again with the pyramids. They're everywhere!

Bless this nest

at least 100 more mounds within the city.

Archaeologists found the remains of a great wooden house on top of Monk's Mound. They think this was the home of Cahokian rulers. The 5,000-square-foot wooden house would have been larger than the original White House. (Apparently, Cahokians thought more highly of their rulers than we do of our presidents.) There's also a gigantic plaza in front of the pyramid. Thousands upon thousands of people could easily have fit into it, and this plaza was built around the year 1000. No one is exactly sure what went on in the plaza.

It shows no signs of being a ball court. The Cahokians played gambling games with sticks and rocks, but they didn't have ball games with rubber balls like the Olmecs and Maya.

Who's Buried in Cahokia's Tomb?

Because the Cahokians left no written records, it's been difficult for archaeologists to decipher their history. Some researchers believe that it's possible that a great ruler emerged in Cahokia, someone like King Pakal of the Maya, who went on a building spree and erected the huge plaza in front of the pyramid. (Somebody must have been in charge!) Archaeologists think that they may have discovered this Cahokian leader's tomb. They found the skeleton of a man laid to rest on a blanket of 30,000 shells in the shape of a falcon. (That's a good sign.) Tucked around him were the bodies of six young men and women laid out like servants. (We're getting warmer!) The tomb was stockpiled with many treasures, including bundles of 1,000 perfectly made arrows. Fifty-three young women were also buried nearby.

Sounds like a king's tomb to me!

Cahokian ruins are so impressive that later European settlers said the city couldn't have been built by ancient people who were here before Columbus. Ben Franklin said the Spanish had built it. The Spanish said the ancient Romans did it. Still others thought that one of the lost tribes of Israel built the mysterious city. Today, archaeologists are almost sure that it was ancient Americans themselves who built Cahokia. There

OK, so I was wrong about the Cahokians. But I still did all that stuff with electricity and made eyeglasses! Top that!

Talk to the hand, Ben.

is no evidence whatsoever that the builders came from anywhere else.

Legends of Cahokia

Archaeologists believe that the Cahokians might have worshiped a sun god. Cahokians studied the movement of the sun so they would know when to prepare the crops. They constructed an elaborate circle of wooden poles in their plaza to mark the sun's movements. This "Woodhenge" is thought to be some sort of a calendar, like Stonehenge, the famous ancient stone site in England.

To learn more about the Cahokians, archaeologists have been studying the legends of the Natchez people, which were written down by French explorers in the 1700s. The Natchez also built great mound cities in the Mississippi Valley, about 200 years after the rise of Cahokia.

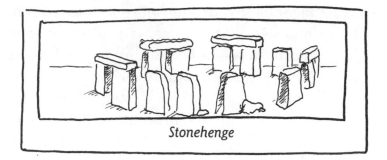

Stonehenge

Woodhenge

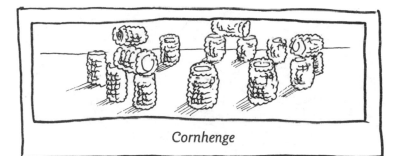

Cornhenge

Roachhenge

Natchez legends are full of references to a great and glorious past. (Of course, if you're going to bother creating a legend, you may as well make it great and glorious!) Many other groups of people living in the eastern United States also have stories about a magnificent golden city of the sun. Archaeologists think that all these legends may be about Cahokia.

According to Natchez legends, the great mounds of Cahokia were built by a group of slaves called Stinkards. Life for the Stinkards stunk. The ruler of Cahokia could kill a Stinkard for any reason, and so could one of his nobles.

I, king of Cahokia, take you, Stinkard. . .

However, one tradition gave the Stinkards hope. Every aristocrat, including the king, had to marry a Stinkard. (They may not have *wanted* to marry a Stinkard, but it sure beat the Maya tradition of putting a thorn through your privates!) If the legend is true, and if Cahokians were ancestors of the Natchez, then Cahokia was one long Cinderella story.

Cahokia Mound State Historical Site is in East St. Louis, Illinois. In 1988, Cahokia was named a United Nations World Heritage Site and declared one of the "elite group of cultural and natural landmarks of special importance to the history of humanity."

The Last Millennium:
Round and Round We Go

One thousand years ago, Cahokia was flourishing. Chaco Canyon was bustling. The Maya were still building great cities. The Hohokam people of Phoenix were building huge ball courts. The people of the Pacific Northwest were throwing elaborate feasts and parties. On the Great Plains, ancient Americans still hunted herds of bison on foot. And the European and Arab nations across the ocean were getting restless.

Cap'n, now can we pleeeease invade someplace warm?

Right around the year 1000, Leif Ericksson landed on the tip of the east coast of Canada. Historians believe that he and his Viking crew may have been the first people from another continent to visit America since the ice age. These Vikings didn't stay long. They were gone in less than 20 years. They never learned of Cahokia or Chaco Canyon, much less the Maya or any of the incredible ancient American cities and cultures that we're still learning about. The Vikings barely stayed long enough to make it into the history books — but they were a sign of things to come!

Pyramids,
mounds,
cliff
houses,
art,
glyphs,
CORN!

(How could we ever forget the corn?!) Wow! That's some kind of history you humans have here in ancient America. And to think: It all happened thousands and thousands of years before Christopher Columbus was even knee-high to a cornstalk.

You people not only figured out how to survive but how to express yourselves. (Okay, not exactly *you*, dear reader, but the ancient Americans — and lots of you are their descendants!) Cockroaches have been around for 250 million years, and we still can't figure out a way to get people to quit squashing us with their shoes!

But, hey! What about those Vikings? They sure didn't stick around very long. (Maybe they had to get back home to feed their cats.) Something tells me Leif Ericksson's not going to be the only one doing a cruise to the Americas. I think the ancient Americans may be in for a big surprise. . . . But that's another story!

Bye-bye for now!

See next page for Map Key.

Map Key

Index